THE ART OF WINNING THE BATTLE WITH STUFF

Expert Strategies with Simple Steps Backed by MinimalisticPhilosophy to Build Habits and Master Decluttering for a Stress-Free and Well-Organized Home, Practical Checklists Included

Jacqueline D. Austin

Copyright© 2024 By Jacqueline D. Austin Rights Reserved

This book is copyright protected. It is only for personal use. You cannot amend, distribute, sell, use, quote or paraphrase any part of the content within this book, without the consent of the author or publisher.

Under no circumstances will any blame or legal responsibility be held against the publisher, or author, for any damages, reparation, or monetary loss due to the information contained within this book, either directly or indirectly.

Disclaimer Notice:

Please note the information contained within this document is for educational and entertainment purposes only. All effort has been executed to present accurate, up to date, reliable, complete information. No warranties of any kind are declared or implied. Readers acknowledge that the author is not engaged in the rendering of legal, financial, medical or professional advice. The content within this book has been derived from various sources. Please consult a licensed professional before attempting any techniques outlined in this book.

By reading this document, the reader agrees that under no circumstances is the author responsible for any losses, direct or indirect, that are incurred as a result of the use of the information contained within this document, including, but not limited to, errors, omissions, or inaccuracies.

Manufactured in the United States of America

Interior and Cover Designer: Danielle Rees

Art Producer: Brooke White

Editor: Aaliyah Lyons

Production Editor: Sienna Adams

Production Manager: Sarah Johnson

Photography: Michael Smith

TABLE OF CONTENTS

Introduction 1

Chapter 1: How a Packrat Became a Neatnik 3

    The Craving for Change 5

        Curiosity: The Tempt to Know More 6

        The Fear of Missing Out (FOMO) 6

        Hedonic Adaptation: The Declining Pleasure 7

    The Simple Yet Uncanny Place Where Change Can Begin 7

    Factors that Contribute To Triggering the Dopamine Surge 8

        Visual Cues 8

        Stress Reduction 9

        Completion of a Task 9

        Anticipation & Habit Breaking 9

    Why do the dishes always reach the sink? 9

    The Real Reason Behind Cluttering! 10

Chapter 2: How to Break Your Bond with Waste Rebound 11

    The Booby Trap of Storage Containers 12

    The Hidden Secret Behind Lifestyle Magazines' Cleaning Approach 15

    How Does Decluttering Help You Make a New Best Friend? 16

    But How Can You Become a Minimalist? 16

        Evaluate your purchases 16

        Quality over Quantity 17

        Limit Decor 17

Chapter 3: Practical Tips that Will Help You Declutter Your House 18

    The Dual Forces: Habit & Goal 18

TABLE OF CONTENTS

    Pair Similar Tasks 19

    Daily-Dating Chores 20

    Weekly Dating Chores 20

    Monthly Dating Chores 21

    Seasonal Dating Chores 21

The Personal Mentor of Decluttering that Lived in Your House for Years 21

The Five Alphabets You Need to Keep Your House Clean 24

    Category A tasks 25

    Category B tasks 25

    Category C tasks 25

    Category D tasks 25

    Category E tasks 25

Sort By Category, Not Location: The Kon Mari Method 26

    Clothes 26

    Books 29

    Papers 31

    Komono 33

    The Desperate Need To Hold Onto Disposables and Gifts 35

The Two Ds of Tidying: Discard & Decide 37

The Five Elements Approach 38

    Wood 38

    Fire 39

    Earth 39

    Metal 40

    Water 41

Chapter 4: The Real Goal Is Not To Clean the House But... 43

Task or Treasure 44

Make Your House Force You to Greet 46

Refrain from Passing Your Clutter Burden 47

You Only Need 7 Sets of Loungewear 48
What You Own Must Serve You 50
The Surprising Effect of Taking a Pre-lunch and Pre-dinner Break 51

Chapter 5: How and Why it is Important to Let Go of Unneeded Keepsakes 53

The Joy of Being Surrounded by Things You Love 53
The Downside of Decluttering and Minimalism 55

Chapter 6: The Gifts of Minimalism & Decluttering 56

How Minimalism & Decluttering Will Make You a Magnet of Good Fortune 57
Seven Keys That Will Help You Identify Your Enough for a Minimalistic Lifestyle 58
The Five Psychological Issues that May Hamper Choice Efficacy 60
House Cleaning Services: Pros and Cons 66

Chapter 7: A Comprehensive Checklist to Declutter 67

Pairing Similar Tasks & Prioritizing Needs Over Wants 67
Role of Timers & The Power of Pre-Breaks 68
The Five Alphabet Approach 68
Make it a Family Event & Sort by Category, Not Location! 69
Breaking the Generational Trauma of Clutter 70

Chapter 8: A Comprehensive Checklist to Minimalism 74

The Art of Mindful Purchasing 74
Farewell to Attachments 74
Investing In the Right Q 74
A Minimalistic Wardrobe 75
Incorporating the Five Elements for Reorganizing Your Home 75

Conclusion 79

INTRODUCTION

Life was simpler when hunting for food and avoiding wild animals were our only concerns. Then, we evolved into the most perceptive creatures to stockpile our caves with every irrelevant item that catches our attention.

The worst part about the best way of cleaning is *'there is none.'*

Every book about cleaning that intrigues you at the bookstore, every lifestyle magazine tip you come across, and every checkbox you fill in, none seems to break your bond with rebounded waste.

The clutter tsunami always returns colossal and sturdier. Even efficient moms and superhumans struggle with cluttering. But nobody seems to voice the pain when motivation fades as you finish reading a book about decluttering.

If a cleaning book would have solved your clutter problem, then the need to keep producing decluttering books would be out of the question, and this is why, after 26 years of my existence, I decided to write this book to help pack rats like me to identify the reason for clutter and get rid of it once and for all.

INTRODUCTION

'Disclaimer: If you belong to those efficient mom categories who sweep the whole house sparkling clean in a day, please refrain from reading this book and join my mom for tea.'

This book is written primarily for those who never identify themselves as slobs, not because they do not want to but because they never knew. Until someone they knew, in my case, my mother pointed out how tiring her life had been since I was born. If you think this is all it took to turn on my de-slobification mode, then news flash: 'YOU ARE WRONG!'

I blew my entire five years of education to understand what writing has to give me. Cut off a stable income source to find that one chance to enjoy the thrill of inspiring strangers through my words.

If you think my life has been easy since then, it is a prime time to let go of your rose-tinted glasses. For the past two years, I have been reminded by strangers how ugly of a failure I look like even after completing my post-grad with a CGPA of 9.

I have developed a thick skin since I started being serious about writing. Until someone critiques my words, no other words seem to seep in. Not until I have to pay a hefty price for my cluttering habit.

So, before I dive into how to get rid of your procasticlutter attitude, let us quickly chat about what inspired me to write this book.

CHAPTER 1:
HOW A PACKRAT BECAME A NEATNIK

Growing up, I witnessed my mother screaming at me regularly for keeping my room unclean.

Confession: It was one of my fondest memories. My mother never failed to insult me creatively. Her words were always; 'I will ask the plumber to install a bathtub on your bed,' or 'I will throw you out of this house if you do not change your ways from tomorrow.'

Unfortunately, that tomorrow never came. I never seriously thought about cleaning and always dodged the conversation with my pet phrase; "Artistic people are messy at their being."

At twenty-two years of age, I realized how much of a half-witted person I sounded with this excuse. After completing my master's, I moved out of my house for a clinical internship. Life gave me an opportunity to live with my aunt and made me realize why my mother was so frantic about cleaning.

I still cannot conclude if the decision I took was a poor or a rich one. But with the timeless knowledge I acquired from this subtle couch-surfing phase, I would love to give her all my credit for inspiring me to write this book.

My Aunt is an active alcoholic and a sweetheart. The only unethical trait she had, except poor alcohol intake, is that she never could convince herself to keep her house clean.

Part of the blame belongs to her increased rate of alcohol intake, which led to poor nerve control, and a substantial part of the blame lies in her nature of dealing with the work later.

I, being a master procrastinator with undiagnosed ADHD, have no right to comment on her. But considering her infamous packrat habits, I moved to her house a month earlier. Just so, I could adapt to the surroundings of my new home. Not the external environment but the internal atmosphere.

For the initial weeks, I hardly cared about the thick layer of dust in the dining room, the mud-covered shoe racks, how the smell of her black-tiled bathroom always made my stomach retch, and how every night the creative insults of my mother echoed in my ears.

One afternoon, as I lay on my bed flipping through an old magazine of bedroom décor, I realized my bed was organized. I abruptly sat up and noticed my surroundings. The whole room still felt as if it was recently ravaged, but my bed was pristine, with fresh sheets tucked neatly at the corners and comfy cushions that were tempting.

As I kept staring at the bedsheet like a possessed individual ready to be exorcized, I realized that the person who kept the bed clean was me. What is more shocking is that I have been doing this since I started living as a guest.

I did not know how to deal with this foreign feeling. Was it happiness, accomplishment, or the urge to mail a picture of my clean bed to my mom to make it framed in her bedroom?

At that moment, I could not identify the exact reason for such an improvement in my habit. But I vividly recall that scene now and often, and the aftermath still surprises me.

Another incident that contributed to turning me into a neatnik was an early lunch.

One summer afternoon, when the leaves were still green and time melted under the cerulean skies, she cooked my favorite white chicken stew. The aroma of the authentic spices made me ditch my family's quotidian lunchtime.

I asked my aunt if I could have an early lunch, and she agreed.

She was sipping on her drink in broad daylight as she served my plate, and the moment I took the first bite, I gagged out, not because it was mouth-burning hot but because it tasted bitter.

I am still clueless about that unidentified object that I accidentally ate. But it was squishy and was mixed with the white chicken stew.

'Give me a moment to pluck my tongue out as I recall that memory.'

This incident has scarred me more than my absurd high school relationships. After a full-fledged discussion with my aunt, asking her not to drink during cooking, I chose peace over rebellion.

She followed my advice for two days and returned to her routine on the third. I started being cautious about what I ate, drank, or allowed my body to intake. I cleaned my bottles and dishes and took an hourly stroll to the kitchen to check her cooking ingredients.

While I managed to thrive in that chaotic whirlwind, I was grateful not to get hospitalized, even after pulling such a great stunt at that early lunch.

My breakthrough came when I lost a requisite paper for my internship. As a result, I could not obtain my internship certificate. Three months of tedious effort, putting in 16 hours a day at work went to complete waste.

I bawled my eyes out for a month but did not give up on fighting the administration. The more they ignored me to address my problem, the more furiously I cleaned the house. Within a week, my cousin termed me a clean freak, and I discovered that my aunt had a white-tiled bathroom, not black.

This period of obnoxious cleaning ushered a significant change in my life. I started being less passive-aggressive, my sleep improved, my overthinking faded, and my pet phrase changed from; 'Artistic people are messy at their being' to 'Artistic people know creative ways to clean.'

The process of creating something extraordinary from scratch will always be messy. Our homes are a testament to it.

As we age, so does every corner of our home. The clutter evolves at every stage of our life. The walls of our room witness us in tears, see us greet life with bright smiles, and become the best companion an individual can ask for.

This delightful realization hit after flipping through the pages of every decluttering book to keep my aunt's house clean.

Understanding the essence of having a creative mess unique to every family and home made me compelled to share with you the joy, benefits, and peace that come gift-packed the moment you decide to declutter your life.

Whether you are an aspiring neatnik, an experienced clean freak, or a packrat who happens to stumble on the book after the weekend spirits.

This book will become your confidante, not because of the cleaning tips, effective tactics, and popular opinions I jot down after reading every clean guru's bible, but because it will help you identify the root cause of cluttering, break your bond with the waste rebound and win the battle against stuff.

The Craving for Change

As humans evolved from hunting animals to fishing clients, the privilege of sleeping on soft cushions, a hot supper, and 24/7 electricity has stopped us from being astonished.

As a result, we always look for ways where these necessities will become a challenge. I guess that explains the constant craving to shift to a different country, city, town, or mountain.

The bliss that serene nature and the thrill of the new brings is incomparable to the constant commotion of words. But, even after running back and forth from greeting necessities and stripping them off, change never seems to match the pace of our living.

Every individual craves a change in their life. Whether you are a billionaire, a thriving entrepreneur, or belong to the gentlefolk group trying to make ends meet, the struggle to break an instilled belief and build a life-changing habit is always wearying.

Our mind throws roadblock after roadblock to make us stick to the known, and the three most common factors that keep us trapped in the loop of craving constant change are **Curiosity, FOMO, and Hedonic Adaptation.**

Before you toss out this book after reading another weighted term, let us get familiarized with the meaning of these three alienated words and how each of them is connected to our need to crave change.

Curiosity: The Tempt to Know More

'Curiosity killed the cat;' the phrase is not only for people who find a thrill in knowing every detail of their surroundings but also for people who aspire to become a clean freak.

Securing the first spot in the weekend sale and claiming the ceramic cracked vase from a fellow shopper will always be a favorite sport to partake in, but what about the colorful plant pots quietly living in your attic? Will they live their purpose in this life?

I understand you have never seen such a unique craft, not one that is reattached after being cracked. You need to admire the craftsmanship and show it to your people. It will eventually make you the talk of the town or the prime topic at tea parties.

The vase will serve you in many ways, some that I can never comprehend. Yet before you convince yourself to enjoy the beauty of that piece, you will catch yourself standing at another weekend sale, grabbing the next hyped item.

As long as we are alive, the world will never run out of our creative artifacts. **To become the center of attention, why fill our homes with things that create tension?** If you say the fear of missing out on living your life, that will bring me to the next factor responsible for craving change **FOMO.**

The Fear of Missing Out (FOMO)

You might have heard the famous phrase from 'Dead Poets Society' by Robert Sean Leonard. I went to the woods because I wanted to live deliberately. I wanted to live and suck out all the marrow of life. To put to rout all that was not life, and not when I had come to die, discover that I have not lived.

To put it in simpler terms, Neil Perry (the fictional character of Robert) did not just want to go through the motions of life. He wanted to be intentional and make conscious choices about how and where he spent his energy and time. He wanted to experience life in a rich and meaningful way, getting rid of anything unimportant or unfulfilling so that he could not feel that he had not lived when he reached the end of his days.

Who knew in 1989 that Neil Perry was subtly addressing decluttering and minimalism?

The world does not cease to revolve as you sleep. People like us from another part of the world wake up and chase the items you did while you were awake.

To highlight my point, you will miss out on myriad items even if you run at laser speed.

You will not be able to get your hands on every unique stuff this world owns. That's the reality, so why do you want to ripen out all your hair in ceasing the next great shopping deal? If you choose to argue with the thrill the new brings. I will make you rethink your decision with the final point of escaping the vicious cycle of craving change Hedonic Adaptation.

Hedonic Adaptation: The Declining Pleasure

As voodoo as the term sounds, the meaning of it is that simple. Hedonic Adaptation is our response to the new. The thrill of having the new subsides as we stuff our houses with the latest. As a result, we get trapped in the endless loop of procuring exclusive items, hoping to be struck by that electrifying feeling again.

Decluttering and a minimalistic approach toward life help us satiate our savage thirst for quantity over quality, free us from the fleeting pressure of chasing trends, and make us understand and appreciate the inherent value of our truest possessions.

When you begin decluttering, you might feel paralyzed by the clutter rebound. But if you dare to shift your focus, adjust your frames, and start seeing life with a minimalistic attitude. You will realize that the change you crave can begin in a simple yet uncanny place you never thought of; YOUR HOME.

The Simple Yet Uncanny Place Where Change Can Begin

Home is where our existence begins. Even a vagabond once had a home. Like charity, Change also begins at home. Anybody with a significant amount of money and intention can invest in a house and start a family.

But only a few can truly make a family thrive without losing their sanity at the clutter that comes inevitably.

The household you were raised in does not determine the degree of clutter your future house will bring, but it will help shape your perspective towards the clutter built.

I was fortunate to be born in a house and to a mother whose prime thoughts revolved around cleaning, having ten dogs, three aquariums, and rescuing a new creature every other day. She never let us understand the amount of clutter these furry companions made.

But when I was forced to live with my aunt and nursed their new rescued labrador, I understood how much litter a pet can produce, if not trained well.

I could stop my aunt for a day or two to get a hold of her packrat habits, but training a full-grown dog in 3 days was a nightmare for me.

The outcome? I cleaned rigorously, day and night, shouting at my cousin to buy dog diapers, crying out silent tears, and worst, developing a hatred towards my favorite animal category.

I knew I needed to change my ways. I had to become more efficient at cleaning and seek advice from my all-rounder mom to help me tackle the multiplying mess.

I could not accept that I was developing feelings for dogs that were not synonyms of Love. But just like the fine performers struggle to break free or build habits necessary to become the ace. I found myself brawling to switch to the mindset of cleaning 24/7.

When you begin your cleaning journey, your home acts as a reflection. It impacts your habits, routines, mental space, and mindset of what kind of individual you can become.

Having a half-tidy home will double your efficiency rather than a ransacked house. Yet, after knowing this valuable advice, we will still find ourselves waiting for the dopamine surge to sweep our floor clean.

Have you ever wondered what other odd factors trigger the reward system of cleaning?

In the following pages, let's have a quick look at them.

Factors that Contribute To Triggering the Dopamine Surge

Several factors contribute to triggering the reward system of cleaning. Dopamine leads the list as long as we humans exist with blooming emotions.

Every individual operates uniquely, and so do our emotions. Some clean when sad, and some wipe off each speck of dust when angry. Some clean to impress, and some when they can no longer stand the pile of laundry in their way.

You might have caught yourself relating to one or the other. But, one factor that creates an equal amount of shame and guilt in every neuro-divergent individual is when a stranger or guest points at our house mess.

The dopamine surge after someone audaciously uses their pointy fingers will always be unmatchable. They can never comprehend how much you have struggled to keep your house tidy, how many hours you stress about the multiplying waste and they will never be bothered to know about it.

But their words will always force us to become neatniks, and sooner we will catch ourselves ranting about our inefficiency. If you think that's the only factor that raises our dopamine levels, let me share the real reason behind my sudden improvement in behavior at my aunt's house. The driving objective that forced me to keep my bed clean.

Visual Cues

I have heard so many tales of how my aunt struggled to clean that I subconsciously trained and commanded my mind to have a clean space when I decided to live with her.

Our mind always finds cues to shift our attention from clutter. I have never seen a person desperately looking for garbage unless they need to use a dustbin.

Organized, clean spaces spark a sense of calm and well-being. This is why we humans subconsciously train ourselves to keep the most used space clean, for example, the bed, but struggle to deal with the mess of the other parts of the house.

So, next time you are stressed about facing another clutter heap, try to find more ways to use that space.

Stress Reduction

When we are under stress, our brain seeks control over our lives. As a result, many people start cleaning obsessively.

The satisfaction and relief after exercising our supremacy in our abode are unreal.

I read somewhere on the internet that we can't control what life throws at us but we can control what we own in our home. Some studies also suggest that women's stress levels are directly proportional to the amount of stuff in their home. Homemakers and Housewives can relate.

The kind of spaces you prefer to spend most of your time on impacts your thoughts. That's why housewives often tend to rely on cleaning homes when they feel anxious.

A happy wife equals a happy life. So, next time you see your partner grumpy, it's time to complete the task assigned to you.

Completion of a Task

I've never seen a person crying over a perfectly completed task unless they can't get any benefit out of it or it is done in the wrong way.

Task completion releases the happy hormone dopamine while reducing the stress hormone cortisol. It makes us feel accomplished and puts meaning into our lives.

House cleaning is an excellent way to feel instant accomplishment. The little spaces we nag about the most while cleaning bring us the most joy once completed.

Anticipation & Habit Breaking

The feeling of getting rid of our monotonous routine and changing our lives 360 degrees has crossed every individual's mind at least once. As an aftermath, we often clean the entire house to fill up the hollowness.

The visualization of a perfectly polished floor, sparkling kitchenware, and aromatic ambiance entices us to such an extent that until and unless our bodies refuse to move, we keep tidying every corner of our rooms.

The sense of anticipation will always be a driving factor for us to clean, but once the dopamine abates, we will catch the dishes quietly marching to our kitchen sink.

> **Why do the dishes always reach the sink?**

Hate to break the cruel truth. But in real life, Harry Potter depends on himself to do his dishes.

We were muggles, are muggles, and we will always be muggles dreaming of belonging to Hogwarts. Even the most skilled VFX artist can only create an illusion of clean dishes or make your wardrobe look like it has not survived a battlefield. The keyword is 'an illusion.'

The only trick that can truly make those dishes disappear or those clothes pressed and folded is using your own hands.

You need to roll up your sleeves and scrub each greasy dish to make it squeaky clean irrespective of the morning rush. You need to gather the piles of dirty clothes scattered throughout your room and put them in the washing machine with the detergent to enjoy the magic of fresh laundry. You need to wipe the countertops each day after every meal to make them sparkling clean.

You need to water your plants regularly to keep them alive for longer periods. You need to empty the trash each week to avoid the foul odor and uninvited pests in your home. You need to change your sheets and liners periodically to maintain the freshness of a clean bed. You need to mop your floors, organize misplaced objects, scrub the windows, polish the mirrors of your home, and groom your pets often to make your house look immaculate. You need to deep clean your house each month to prevent accumulating waste and you need to keep making significant cleaning progress every day to not let the clutter build.

There's no potion, spell, or invisible cloak that will make clutter disappear in seconds until you want to weed out the real reason for cluttering to reach your goal of a spotless home.

The Real Reason Behind Cluttering!

The NY Times Bestseller Author Charles Duhigg was the first to make me dive deep into the 'Power of Habit.' Through his habit loop, I decoded the clutter cycle and ceased it once and for all.

Imagine this, for every spoon of Nutella you scoop, you wash it in the sink and keep it where it belongs. Every time you complete cooking, you wash the extra spoons, and bowls used during meal preparation.

Once you complete laundering the essentials, fold them and keep them in the closet. When you wake up in the morning, you don't exit your room without making the bed. After every meal, you quickly wash off the plates before retiring for the day. Do you think the dishes will still find their way to the sink?

If you answer yes, then you are right. The dishes will march up to the kitchen sink, but the amount of it will reduce drastically.

Even if this idea seems feasible as you read, chances are there will be days when you will fail to keep up with the momentum, and before you can comprehend, you will be greeted again by that one clingy lover; Rebound.

So, how do you make your cleaning habits irresistible and keep rebound at bay? In the next chapter, I'll help you to break your bond with waste rebound.

CHAPTER 2:

HOW TO BREAK YOUR BOND WITH WASTE REBOUND

Rebound can be compared to the blindsiding need to connect with something heart-fluttering after a stupid breakup. Even if we cross our hearts and hope to die as we begin our healing or cleaning journey, we tend to get enticed at the first thought of experiencing the comfort of our old habits, much like the thrill of a whirlwind romance.

I have always been a blessed one. So, I have only rebounded with all things toxic, be it Clutter or Partner. Getting rid of clutter is much easier than getting rid of the latter.

Clutter has always been smitten by me. When I lived at my aunt's house, Clutter seemed to be head over heels in love with me. Even if I cleaned every hour, every minute, I still found myself being roommates with it.

Until I realized that it was not only my aunt and her beloved dog but also my cousin who helped Clutter to have a space of its own.

Now, before you count my cousin as a packrat, let me tell you, she was not cluttering consciously. It was the unconscious habits that we both built throughout our lives that made me re-greet with Rebound.

How did I fix that? I tackled the first habit or rather items that caught my attention, 'Containers.'

The Booby Trap of Storage Containers

The source of false hope began the day containers were invented. Containers are helpful, but only when used mindfully. Unfortunately, the urge to decorate every space of our rooms with containers rules out the meaning of '**limit**' from our homes.

Only the convenience and euphoric feeling of fancy jam jars and take-out containers seem to add meaning to our quotidian life.

The house where I grew up has a small storage section right beside the staircase. The space is so dark and above the ground level that it looks like a black hole on the wall.

Except for my mother and her containers, nobody has ever dared to enter that haunted space, and there is a valid reason for me to call it spooky. Once, our pet playfully entered it during his periodic zoomies. It took him several minutes to come out from that place with his ears folded and his tail pressed between his legs.

It has been 8 years since this incident, and we still have no clue who he saw inside that dark cavity that made a full-grown dog wince like a puppy.

I would not be surprised if my brother rings up and informs me that a box monster has taken its revenge on my mom. She breathes, lives, and probably secretly eats her meals in those containers. But, even after 27 years of my mother collecting boxes like Pokémon cards, space never seems to run out of that little dark corner of our house.

I decoded the secret after I read Dana K. White's book "How to Manage Your Home Without Losing Your Mind." She enlightened me with the knowledge that the word containers means **to contain,** and this was when I realized how my mother efficiently managed to keep all her containers intact in that black hole.

The thought of cleaning always creates the image of an organized space. As we dive deep to understand the nuances of an organized home, containers block our vision.

Have you ever wondered what attracts us to containers? Is it the shape, color, or the pleasure of contentment it creates that enchants us to have at least one in our homes? Here are the four psychological sides that containers trigger in us.

Four sides of us that inspire us to become kidnappers of containers.
....

✶ **The Daydreamer:**

We constantly visualize living in our ideal state to such a great extent that we refuse to accept our present. As a result, every container we come across looks like a necessity for future events. Yet, when the time arrives, the first containers we use are the regular ones or stride to the market to get us a new set.

* **The Guilty Spender:**

I would be surprised if you never spent an entire check on an item and realized later that it would never be able to serve you in any way.

Shopaholics can relate to the above statement better. The temptation to decorate your home with those fancy ceramic vases coupled with the sweet false hope of the salesperson always makes us go through a bad trip once we realize our houses have become an antique shop of empty hopes.

* **The Art & Craft Freak:**

If you were a junk collector like me, you already would have a fair idea of what I am about to say; 'that idea of craft will produce more junk than beauty.'

Unless you have a child enrolled in school, none of the containers will ever be put to use, and even if you did have a child, that child will outgrow your ideas to upcycle those plastic molds.

There's a little art and craft freak living inside each of us, but that should never become an excuse to store clutter in our homes. I also tend to collect seashells when I visit the beach, only to make myself stressed during cleaning and earn an extra earful of insults from my mom.

I am still searching for a good enough reason to not get emotionally attached to these fatuous charms. However, I found a way to effectively create space for my every new sea-shell collection.

* **The Hoarder:**

Being blessed to be chosen as the secret keeper of all my friends' group I was entitled to play the part of Hedwig in middle school among all the potential couples who belonged to a strict home.

'My boyfriend gave me a rose during recess. Could you hide it inside your bag? Somebody gave me a Secret Santa note. Could you keep it for a day or two?'

My family has always been lenient when it comes to boys. They have such immense trust in their daughter that until and unless I straight up introduce someone as my boyfriend. Nobody ever bothered about any hearsay. The leverage of this leniency was exercised by my friends to turn me into their love lockers.

Consequence? An uncountable number of letters, arts and crafts, and boxes and boxes of stuffed toys ogling their eyes out at me.

I felt sad about the breakups but more anguished to never consciously force them to take back their clutter. Even if we get rid of things that do not serve us anymore, there are items we cannot seem to part ways from. So, how do we discard those items that hold a great deal for us?

CHAPTER 2

I will discuss the trauma generational clutter can bring in the later chapters and which keepsakes deserve a place in our lives or our homes but for now, here is the key to breaking free from the booby trap of storage containers.

'Start living in the present.'

Yes, you read it correctly. That's the only key to breaking free of the booby trap of storage containers. It is good to have a picture of an ideal home in your mind. But to create one, you should let go of what does not serve you anymore.

A great way to get a hold of your container obsession is by understanding the true meaning of the advice given by author Dana K. White, that a container means to contain. They come with a specific dimension to store a certain amount of your belongings.

You already have enough space to store your belongings at your house, and if you are marching to Ikea for a new shelf or furniture, stop and ask yourself, 'Is there space in your home to display it, or are you going to figure it out once you become a neatnik?'

Launch mini-campaigns to go through your belongings and categorize them into two categories, the least favorite and the most favorite. After you are done, categorizing, find one functional box that can gulp your every favorite belonging and one that can eat your least favorite items.

Once done, bid farewell to those least favorites so that they can come and find you again in a more functional rather than aesthetic way.

Speaking of functionality, let us unravel the Lifestyle magazine's **secret** to cleaning approach.

The Hidden Secret Behind Lifestyle Magazines' Cleaning Approach

Who does not want to have a home with sparkling countertops, color-coordinated shelves, and minimalistic decor? A home that screams you are living inside your dream lifestyle magazine.

Those shiny pages allure us, convince us to follow and attain the idea of aesthetics that we forget the role of functionality in surviving.

Aesthetics are great, but only on paper and on social media platforms. Life demands functionality in every aspect of our being. Following those easy-to-stick magazine-friendly tips will only make you cross paths with rebounded waste.

Then why do the homes look so perfect on those pages? Easy. They create a setting only with the necessary items, and with the help of professional photographers, they make magic happen.

They solely focus on aesthetics over functionality. You will be convinced that the blue storage will perfectly fit all your belongings. But once you welcome it to your home, the size will be a mismatch, while the color of your walls will make that electrifying blue an eye sore.

Then how can we understand which item to invest our time, energy, and money in? Easy! The items that can serve you in a multifunctional way for all your needs.

A great example of a multifunctional item would be the vintage-style compact nail cutters and reusable chopsticks.

I have a purple box where I keep all the seashells I have collected over the years. When I plan a trip to the beach, I quickly go through the box to return the broken ones or the ones that have become my least favorite.

I walk to the seashore, open the box, and make all the shells greet the sea. Then, I carefully pick the ones that are broken, lackluster, or give me a sense that they miss home, thank them, say my farewell, and send them away with the wave back to their home again.

This is one of my favorite activities at the beach and my little way to not let the clutter multiply. If you ask how I resist the urge to buy a new box? I simply choose a box that I can comfortably fit in my go-to travel knapsack.

Over the years, I have developed feelings for my purple box too. It gives me a sense of protecting my shells and keeping them all intact for months. To thank it, I always feel obliged to carry the box to the sea and all the shells that I have collected throughout my years of traveling.

After all, every being deserves to return to where they belong truly.

It is necessary to draw little boundaries that you can't even cross. This way, you will become adaptable to frequently changing your ways and clarifying your thoughts.

Once you shift your perspective to functionality, make it a boundary to never let anything enter your house premises that is not functional.

Setting essential boundaries in every aspect of your life will help you bid farewell to your cluttering tendencies and introduce you to your new best friend.

How Does Decluttering Help You Make a New Best Friend?

Once you develop the constant urge to declutter, you will be tagged with a new friend, minimalism.

Minimalism is allowing the essential to express who you truly are. Prioritizing, what's necessary. Imagine if we start living in caves.

Do you think the woofer base will be counted as a functional item without electricity?

If a wild beast showed up, everybody would sprint in different directions rather than impressing it with a dance routine.

You can argue with the idea that minimalism means restrictive living, embracing the boring, and stripping the little joys that make our lives worthwhile.

And I would appeal that it's quite the opposite. It will help you to get rid of too many ifs and buts and identify the treasures of life.

A minimalistic approach towards life will not fill you with regrets but will help you to live a life with none.

You'll have a home free of clutter, your custom wish lists every time you shop, an immaculate space for yourself, and a completely personalized wardrobe aligned to your unique style that will never make you run out of good clothes.

But How Can You Become a Minimalist?

Now that I have brainwashed you to embrace the new, here are some initial tips to make you an instant minimalist.

Evaluate your purchases

Social media can be a boon if you correctly use it. I am in the category of people who comment at every reel that it is my last reel of the day and never un-glue my eyes from the screen till the alarm sends the notification that it will ring in 15 minutes.

It has always been an unanswered question whether the media platforms ever served us (the non-influencers) in any way other than the little shots of dopamine hit until I stumbled upon one reel that my friend sent me.

I have taken a mental snapshot, hung it on a billboard over my occipital lobe, and recited it as a mantra on every trip to Target.

The words were simple, but combined with a shopping spree, it became a supernatural weapon. Even my friend, who never seems to run out of cash, saved twice the amount she used to.

The tactic is to question yourself at every purchase; Do you want the item for others to see you have it, or do you want yourself to own it?

This statement will drastically improve your spending habits and give tough competition to Richie Rich.

Quality over Quantity

Imagine being given the choice to speak to someone who will spend two hours boasting about the achievements they have earned in their life and to another person with a 15-minute time frame who will help you plan out your future goals.

Whom would you prefer to talk to and why? Is it the duration that makes you repel from the braggart or the compelling offer that attracts you to add a minute or two with the listener?

Chasing quantity is good if you are thinking of media platforms. Triggering the algorithm with regular updates is better for garnering attention. But to keep them hooked, you will trace your steps back to Quality again.

Shopping centers are similar to social media platforms. They blind us with brightly colored tags. Make us feel supreme for being a bargain hunter in our every purchase and then leave us to suffer the consequence of favoritism.

You might think that the coat will make you more fashionable at your Met Gala moment, but before D-day arrives, you will catch yourself skipping work to buy a green scarf to pair with it.

Investing in quality purchases over quantity will save you more time, space, and money. It is better to own an item that can be paired with ten different outfits than spending your entire paycheck per month to restock your wardrobe.

Limit Decor

How often does it happen when you decide to get only one item to keep as a memory of your first trip and come back home with a bag full of fridge magnets, wooden masks, and meaningless keepsakes that make your home a Pandora's box?

Sure, that hyena mask looks tempting on your trip to Amazon, but does it compliment your Barbie-themed house decoration?

Decorating your space with items that remind you of the phrase fish out of the sea will consume more time to clean than necessary.

The best way to fight the urge to bag every souvenir on your trip is to take a picture to reminisce. Once the dopamine fades, that picture will be the first to line up in your cellphone's recycle bin.

CHAPTER 3:
PRACTICAL TIPS THAT WILL HELP YOU DECLUTTER YOUR HOUSE

In the last chapters, I have shared a comprehensive checklist that will further touch on some new points of decluttering your home but before you need to learn how to maximize the benefits of the dual forces that drive every human being to reach their goal.

The Dual Forces: Habit & Goal

When you are a toddler, you constantly get directed by adults. Wake up, brush your teeth, wash your hands, eat your greens, carefully cross the road, wave goodbye, study...a constant dictatorship.

But once you reach the 'age of why', suddenly, all the adults start to retire from their positions of authority. The wisdom you have in your teenage years makes it difficult for them to exercise their jurisdiction.

Building good habits is quite similar to dictatorship. We beat ourselves to such an extent that our processes to build good habits become the sole obstacle to reaching our goal.

I have never seen an active person grieving over good health but witnessed those with a sedentary lifestyle complain about declining fitness.

Habits are hard to build. I will repeat, **Habits are hard to build.** The sole ingredient that differentiates good habits from bad is hormones.

During the initial stage, the process of building a good habit revolves around cortisol (the stress hormone), which forces one to deal with anxiety to reach dopamine (the happy hormone).

On the other hand, Bad habits are great at playing the part of cupid and directly introduce us to dopamine. This is why we pick up a bad habit in 24 hours but struggle to complete a 15-minute HIIT workout.

When did you last consciously think about the benefits of brushing your teeth regularly?

Until we or someone whimpers on the floor with a toothache or has to schedule a routine dentist appointment, the thought of your teeth's health hardly crosses your mind. But we still put effort into brushing it regularly, once, twice, or sometimes thrice on special occasions.

Unlike in childhood, brushing our teeth does not look like a chore anymore. The reason is that we do not put any conscious effort. Your muscles are trained to follow the routine of brushing; picking up the brush, squeezing the toothpaste, and sticking it inside your mouth.

On the contrary, House cleaning needs constant **conscious effort.** Restricting yourself from the dopamine shots of browsing through the store just for fun needs **discipline,** two challenging yet highly coveted items to reach an individual's ultimate goal.

Think about it; if cluttering your house needs conscious effort and discipline, would you read this book?

No! Right?

You will be hunting for a book that teaches you how to clutter if the world claims clutter is attractive.

The 'goal' will always fall under the category of 'reap,' and to reach you have to 'sow' the essential 'habits.'

But how do you make a good habit irresistible like the bad ones? How can you not put conscious effort into cleaning your house?

In the following pages, I'll guide you through the 5 practical steps that you can implement to declutter your mess and become an authentic minimalist who knows how to part ways with stress.

Pair Similar Tasks
....

The sole reason to sulk in your procasticlutter attitude is to categorize each task individually. Our daily chores are star-crossed lovers. They are connected through a red thread and forced to live separately in the same space.

The reason for their agony is your inability to identify yourself as the matchmaker.

Try to focus and let go of your chore-breaker personality and start playing the part of being their cupid. It is easier to remind yourself to wash the extra cooking utensils as you finish cooking than to wait for the perfect timing.

It is easier to fold the clothes and keep them in the closet after laundering than to wait for Cinderella to send her little mice Gus-Gus and Jaq for help.

When you start pairing similar tasks, you will notice that building and following a regular habit of cleaning is easier. It is the habit of seeing each task separately that makes the essential work look like a chore.

Here's a checklist that will help you identify the power couples of your home.

Daily-Dating Chores

Meal Times + Dish Cleaning

Making Bed + Decluttering Your Desk

Picking Toys + Vacuum Room

Wiping Countertops + Mopping Floors

Weekly Dating Chores

Vacuuming Furniture + Organizing Shelf

Taking out The Trash + Cleaning the Containers

Watering Plants + Plucking the Dead Leaves.

PRACTICAL TIPS THAT WILL HELP YOU DECLUTTER YOUR HOUSE

Laundering Clothes + Organizing Closet

Monthly Dating Chores

Organizing Bills + Clipping Them

Cleaning rugs + Vacuuming Carpets

Wiping Mirrors + Scrubbing Windows

Bathroom Floors + Toilet Clean

Seasonal Dating Chores

Laundering Seasonal Clothes + Packing Off Season Ones

Mowing the lawn + Sweeping the Porch

You get the idea. Once you understand what chore comes after, building a regular habit of cleaning will never be bemusing. You will often deal with only one task from the pairs I listed. Why? Because your indoor plant will not have dead leaves to shed every week.

The only aspect that can hinder your progress in completing a task is your speed of tackling it, for which I would ask you to rely and take the help of the personal mentor living in your house for years; TIMERS.

The Personal Mentor of Decluttering that Lived in Your House for Years

One of the biggest challenges faced by humankind is managing time effectively. For this reason, the Egyptians invented the water clock, and just like water, time flowed, waiting for nobody.

It becomes your biggest enemy if you ignore it and your best friend when you learn to match steps with time, but house cleaning never seems to socialize well with time.

Then how do we persuade them to befriend each other? Easy. Take the help of your decluttering mentor, Timers.

I first discovered the power of timers in completing a task when I worked an odd job that required me to put in eleven hours. As I dragged myself back home, I was greeted by a new set of clutter, and as I cleaned my way to move to my favorite task; crafting words. I felt exhausted as the clock struck 'time out for the day.'

I spent weeks hoping to become a multitasker. But as the days of the calendar advanced, I found myself sobbing, frustrated, blaming my family for burdening me with the vows that were never mine to take.

I desperately looked for ways to become a multitasker. I tried to complete 3 similar tasks at once, kept taking little detours around the house to detect any misplaced objects and organize them, redesigned my entire room with little sticky to-do lists, and yet never seemed to chalk out enough time to sit and write.

The to-do list kept lengthening. If I wrote five big tasks to tackle, it multiplied into eight by morning, eleven by afternoon, and twenty-two by night.

None of the multitasking tricks worked, none except two and I would not categorize them under the multitasking tools I found on the internet because my high school friend and a random social media reel helped me understand the true meaning of multitasking.

One night, after I crawled back home from my job, I refused to clean. I went straight to my home and sat on my bed aimlessly. Nobody in my aunt's house seemed bothered about my decision as they were already accustomed to living in messy surroundings.

But after a few minutes, her furry companion started meddling with the litter, causing me to eat back my words. I quickly got up and started scrubbing the floor. The moment I finished my frustration morphed into anger towards the dog.

I could not tolerate even the sight of him, and as much as he inched near me to be petted, I shooed him away.

That night, I bawled my eyes, and the guilt of shooing the dog away made me gloomy. I felt terrible. I desperately needed someone to tell me what more I could do. Or what wrong I was doing?

Surprisingly, my high school friend called me that night, and as we nagged each other about our day, he casually mocked, 'Why don't you wear a watch while cleaning?' That's when it clicked. I could ask clocks to help me and use timers to speed up my process.

I felt powerful. The clarity that I could be more efficient putting a timer on made me feel like I possessed infinity stones. For a week, I started being the most productive self of mine.

The thought of an ongoing timer at the back of my head thrilled me. I started to look forward to cleaning. As I walked home from work, I smiled like a loon, imagining myself cleaning the clutter.

A lady on the bus once asked me if something happened, and I answered, 'I am just happy at the thought that I had to clean my room.' As absurd as it sounded to that lady. It was the truth. I was delighted. Cleaning became a solo mini-marathon that I competed and won.

The hours of my week-offs never seem to get engulfed by time anymore. I feel energized, happy, and productive. I started my website, updated blogs, and wrote stories, news, and articles. I thrived. Lived.

But as time flowed, I noticed a change. Time again started to run faster than me, and no matter how much I tried, the timer always won.

I tackled tasks as much as I could but sulked back to a load of crap as soon as the timer went off. I could not understand what made the clocks enraged at me that I kept failing every day.

I started questioning my aunt's family 'How much load of crap a nuclear family can produce?' I even went to the clockmaker and asked if my timer was broken, but nobody seemed to have an answer to my questions.

Slowly, the thought of timers made me anxious, my ADHD escalated, and I often found myself glued to my cell phone screen, spending hours after hours, letting the clutter build.

This is when social media again proved how much power it holds. I followed one account that used to share study techniques when I pursued my master's degree. I never applied those techniques in my studies, but I enjoyed the aesthetics of the posts.

One night, as I scrolled through the media, the term Pomodoro Technique flashed on my screen. I skipped it, and after a few minutes, another reel had the same term, and after a few minutes, there was another.

The term revolved in my feed for so many reels that it forced me to swipe back and check the definition on the Internet.

The Pomodoro Technique is a time management method popular among students who want to ace their studies. In the late 1980s, Francesco Cirillo developed this technique for increasing the levels of concentration.

He used a tomato-shaped kitchen timer during his university days to manage extended periods of concentration. In this technique, students are advised to study for 25 minutes and take a five to ten-minute break. Once four rounds of Pomodoro (twenty-five minutes) are completed they can take a prolonged break of 20-30 minutes.

I applied it to my cleaning rituals but with the twist of not using the breaks in between. When I consciously put in the effort every 25 minutes, I understood how big of a difference it made and how energized I felt throughout the day.

I never needed the breaks as when I clean my house, I hardly care about resting. The short 25-minute timers were perfect for me to analyze which task was engulfing my maximum hours and without the breaks in between I realized that I was procrastinating on a single task and not cleaning.

Household chores are similar to your semester syllabus. To-do lists are the indexes of the chapters your home holds. Setting a short timer made me consciously put effort at every interval and made me discover that folding the laundry needs only 10 minutes, not thirty.

Timers are great if you want to increase your efficiency at any work; always set a timer even if it's unnecessary; it will help you keep track of your time, improve your concentration, and help you understand how much time you need to tackle one category of clutter at your home.

Additionally, short-timers also prevent burnout regardless of your house's dimension.

Every person in this world does the same household work, be it any ethnicity, race, or caste; the core of our household chores remains identical. The dimension of your home and the quality of clutter determines how many hours you need to clean each corner of your room.

Make a personalized timer list unique to your home.

The Five Alphabets You Need to Keep Your House Clean

Let's face it! There were days when one category of clutter grew as if it was in a growth spurt overnight. Instead of 10 minutes, it takes 30, even forty-five minutes of complete concentration to clean the mess.

That one category consumes so much of your time that you are forced to skip some of the points on your to-do list and shift it to another day.

Unlike a chapter in a book, household chores multiply Every. Single. Day, and before you know it, you have a bundle of to-do lists slowly consuming another week of your month.

It becomes a constant loop of doing a three-week-old task and never finding enough time for the present one.

I felt trapped in time. Each week, I was cleaning, and even though I could chalk out a few hours to write, I knew that I still had three tasks on my list to complete. The anticipation affected my productivity.

I was not ready to jeopardize my hours of researching and writing to tackle one task that would consume God knows how many hours.

So, I started procrastinating at my work again. I read books but never wrote a line, watched shorts, but never consciously looked for solutions. I was fed up with the paraphrased bits of advice that every decluttering book made.

None made a difference. No tips were personalized enough to help me deal with my clutter. Then, one fine day, I came across a time productivity book 'Eat That Frog' by Author Brian Tracy.

According to Mr. Brian Tracy, each task is a frog and one should aim to eat the ugliest frog first. It also emphasizes the idea of ranking your tasks using the ABCDE letters.

I applied it to my projects, and it worked. I decided to use it for my household chores, and it produced pure wonder.

When we clean, we often feel paralyzed at concluding which clutter needs immediate attention. Countless decluttering books emphasize completing the easy task first. But the trick lies not in doing the easy task but in knowing which clutter is the ugliest frog in your home.

Here's a detailed description for deciphering and implementing the ABCDE method in your household chores.

- **Letter A:** Clutter that once dealt can drastically affect your home's ambiance.

- **Letter B:** Household chores that you must finish by the end of the day.

- **Letter C:** Extra chores that will make you feel a little more productive.

- **Letter D:** Acronym for easy tasks that can be delegated.

- **Letter E:** Household tasks that you can eliminate.

As you begin your decluttering journey, you will feel alone. But it often turns out decluttering was never a solo journey.

The people around us can prevent our space from being a zone of clutter. Why waste your time solo cleaning and not make it an event instead? Gather everybody who contributed to the clutter built.

Here is my list of household chores ranked as per each alphabet.

Category A tasks

A1: Cooking Meals.

A2: Laundering the Essentials.

A3: Wiping Counters, Tabletops & Sweeping Floors.

Category B tasks

B1: Washing Dishes.

B2: Making the Bed.

B3: Folding the Laundry.

B4: Emptying the Trash Bin.

Category C tasks

C1: Dusting the Furniture.

C2: Mopping the Floors.

C3: Organizing my Closet.

C4: Getting rid of the age-old coffee stain on my bookshelf.

C5: Watering my indoor plants.

Category D tasks

D1: Requesting my teen cousin to fill the water bottles.

D 2: Requesting my mother to re-decorate the mementos shelf.

D 3: Requesting my aunt to arrange the previous bills and sort the new ones.

D 4: Asking my brother to stop being a cluttered case.

D 5: Requesting my father to help me repair the broken swing.

Category E tasks

E1: Mowing the lawn

E2: Cleaning the Porch

E3: Washing the car

When we categorize our tasks, we know exactly how many tasks belong to us and how many we can ask for help. There's nothing wrong in asking for help, and there will be times when you will be astonished by how skilled your family is at quickly completing their assigned tasks.

You can shuffle the ranking of task categories as per priority or create a new one. In my case, I am terrible at decorating the shelf with mementos.

Every piece seems to stare at me with starry eyes pleading to be the center of attention, and if I force myself to go for aesthetics and pack away the ugly. The thought of them living in the attic after suffering my cruel judgment haunts me for days.

As witchy as it sounds, I believe every inanimate object in my home seems to have a life of its own, and I was no one to hold them back to live their true purpose.

So, once I clean my desk or the shelf, I always ask my mom to re-decorate it. That way, I maintain my relationship with each category of items that I own and even keep my organizational paralysis far off.

Sort By Category, Not Location: The Kon Mari Method

If you have ever cleaned your house, even once, you might have noticed yourself cleaning the same category of items at different locations. Every house owns a category of items unique to them. By unique, I mean the amount of the item.

Imagine there are two people: we will call them R and S. R tends to shop at every little or grand event. On the other hand, S likes to read and often bargains with the booksellers to get a better deal.

If they decide to clean, R will find clothes stacked at different places in her home, and S will find old books scattered around. Even if both possess a different category, they will go through these items throughout their cleaning process. And before they make any visible progress. The sun will set.

The New York Times Best Seller Author 'Marie Kondo' advises aspiring declutterers to sort items by category, not location.

In the book The Life-Changing Magic of Tidying Up, she reminded us how we tend to store similar items in different places. As a result, we often spend time organizing and reorganizing multiple items in the same place.

The best way to break this constant loop is following the order Marie Kondo suggests.

Clothes | Books | Papers | Komono | Mementos

Clothes

According to the author and founder of Kon Mari Media, Marie Kondo, clothes are the best category to start decluttering with, as our feelings attached to them vary. If a cloth has served its purpose and no longer brings joy to you, it is better to let go of that item.

When you begin decluttering, select a space and gather all your clothes. Now, spread each item on the floor and examine if it still serves you.

Start with the clothes that you forgot existed in your closet. Do those clothes still fit? If it does, can it be paired in multiple ways? Is it something that you can use immediately? Does that spark joy and happiness?

Questioning yourself will hone your sense of discarding items that no longer serve you. Beginning with items you never knew existed in your wardrobe will refine your sense of purpose and keep decision paralysis at bay.

Make two piles: One to discard and one to keep once you finish categorizing. Get rid of the discard pile immediately. Sell, throw, or donate to a charity, but never to your family. I will discuss later why gifting clothes that are of no use to you can be a burden to your family. But first, focus on discarding the pile immediately. If you delay dealing with the pile, the items will re-influence you to keep them in the closet.

Only keep those clothes you can wear today, tomorrow, and within six months. Seasonal clothes piled for next year will never live their purpose. The weather is erratic. If you choose and decide to wear a particular cloth once the temperature rises or drops, you will forget about the item and instead opt for a new one.

I used to own items in my closet that I never wore. Some I picked because my best friends in high school did. Some with the hope that I will be able to fit in someday when I finally convince myself to lead a healthy lifestyle.

I am still in the convincing phase, and the purple and green yoga mats I purchased are tethered into bits by my rescued dogs. It's good to make plans for a better you, but stacking up your closet in the hope that someday you will finally have a chance to wear that one dress without moving your arms and legs is just pure torture to yourself and your closet.

You can keep only one item that inspires you to be your better self. Clothes stored with the thought of future use never play any part in our lives other than the part of being your hostage.

Using space-saving folding techniques is a smart way to store clothes but to get benefitted you need to learn the right way to store your clothes.

* **The Right Way to Store Your Clothes**

Once you discard what no longer serves you, put serious thoughts into keeping what you own. If you do not think consciously, rebound will soon return to your closet.

Many of us feel we will be left with an empty closet case if we brutally discard every piece of clothing that sparks no joy, especially people with a small closet collection like me. The keyword is 'feel.'

After graduation, the exhilaration of shopping for clothes decreased. Shopping no longer cured my blues. This sudden shift surprised and shocked my dad more than me.

There were no longer periodic doorbells for parcels and constant reminders from Dad to stop spending paychecks on my wardrobe.

I felt content every time I peeked into my wardrobe. The small collection is enough to support me year-round, and learning how to store clothes correctly made it easy to spot any items in one glance.

Some people prefer to store their clothes hung with hangers on clothing rods, but when it comes to storing clothes in your home, space-saving must always be your prime thought.

There are specific ways to fold each item, and learning the accurate method to fold and store each category of your clothes will be a skill you want to pass down for generations.

Here is a list of all categories of clothes and the right way to fold them.

Tops (T-shirts, Sweaters & Button ups)

Two great ways to fold your upper wears are File Fold and Half Fold.

+ **File Fold**

File folds are best for space-saving methods. It keeps your clothes wrinkle-free and ironed for extended periods without eating space in your wardrobe.

Lay your t-shirt front down. Draw an imaginary rectangle from the t-shirt's neck to the bottom. Then, fold one side of the sleeve to the center of the rectangle and fold another side of the sleeve over it.

Now, fold your t-shirt in half, leaving a little space towards the upper part in the direction of your fold, then in half or thirds to make a compact rectangle.

Aim to make it look like a small clutch that you can easily hold on your palm, and always keep your t-shirt upright inside your wardrobe.

+ **Half Fold:**

This technique is effective for thicker items. Lay your clothes front down. Then, fold the T-shirt in half vertically and half horizontally. Mirror the steps in File Fold and keep it stacked one above the other in your wardrobe.

The shape of your thicker item will look similar to a clutch but a broader one.

Pants (Dress Pants, Jeans & Shorts)

+ **Half Leg Fold:**

Lay your pants front up, then fold them vertically, one over the other. Fold the waistband towards your ankle and then fold your ankles towards the waistband. Once done, give a final fold in half or thirds.

+ **Kon Mari Fold:**

Similarly, Lay the front of the jeans up and then fold one leg over the other. Fold the ankle area towards the waistband, leaving a little space at the upper half, and then fold it in half or thirds.

Dresses & Skirts

+ **Fold it in Thirds:**

Lay it flat and then fold it in half lengthwise. Fold the bottom towards the waist. Then give a final fold for making a compact rectangle.

+ **Hangers:**

For garments that wrinkle easily, Author Marie Kondo recommends hanging them using padded hangers to maintain the shape of the garment.

Underwear, Bras & Socks
....

The right way to fold underwear is to fold it half horizontally and then half vertically.

For bras, fold the cups one over the other, then push one pad inside another to create a one-cup bra.

The secret to saving your socks from looking like potato lumps is to fold them in half and then roll them like spring rolls, making them tight and upright. The swirl of the roll should always be facing upward when kept. Another method is to put one sock inside another and then fold it into mini rectangles.

Hats, Caps, Beanies & Scarves:

The best way to store head apparel is by determining the quantity you hold and its essence. Baseball caps of children have a special place in every mom's heart. Determining the volume will help you understand the area of space you need to store them properly.

Some manageable ways to store head apparel are keeping all your beanies in a basket or folding them in little squares. Scarves should be pleated in compact rectangles and stored in sectioned drawers or you can use clothing rods to tie them to add personal taste to your room decoration.

Expensive material hats can be stored using hat rings, boxes, and hooks. Baseball caps on wall hangers in the living room add interest to your decor.

Clothes for Babies

Baby clothes and toddler items like onesies, and swaddle blankets can be folded in half matching the edges, and then folding the apparel into half or thirds to make it a mini or medium size rectangles. You can also choose to roll the onesies to save space in your baby's wardrobe.

One great way to prevent losing baby clothes is by choosing to store identical items together, onesies with onesies, pants with pants. Since the size of baby clothes is smaller than adults one must always focus on hygienic clean spaces, try to store baby closets in an entirely different compartment on your wardrobe.

Books

Unlike clothes, books possess a source of power that taints if not cared for. The books you choose to read reflect your identities. It portrays who you are as a human being. You might have heard the phrase, "You are what you eat." As a reader and writer, I believe 'you are what you read.'

Many might argue this is an absurd ideology, as our tastes vary. But the kind of books you read influence your outlook. It shapes you as an individual and prepares you for life experiences.

Nobody has ever been the same after finishing a book that captivated them. But, when it comes to storing books, we all have ridden the same shuttle of struggling to find enough space in our homes. It is hard to let go of books, especially for those who own a personalized home library.

I could never let go of any books and keep them stacked on my shelves with the hope that I would re-read them once I finished a task, but the task list kept multiplying.

For me, books are the source of my being. I have this contentious belief that the books I buy are meant to find me. Even if I disagreed with the plots and characters, I kept them in my collection. My collection used to be books I adored, books I never wanted to re-read, or books that were an absolute infliction of pain. Every book I would refrain from recommending held a place in my bookshelf.

Aftermath?

I started noticing that the number of unread books kept multiplying. The thought that I might dislike the plotline made me procrastinate and abstain from reading it. But the book covers were pretty. So, I kept adding one after another book to my collection.

Then, one day, Mom sold it to the recycler without my permission. I was furious but later realized that it never really affected me. Books that you would not recommend others to read are the not-to-keep ones.

Think about it. Would you like to give a friend something that you disliked? You can always choose to share the gist of the story without spoilers or the ideas associated with the non-fiction books. If it does not spark their interest, why bother keeping it anyway?

Now, there are books you struggle to part ways with or books that make you the most puzzled; study, and reference books. Here is a quick list of how to say farewell to each genre of book and make space for the ones that remain and make up your collection.

Start by dividing your books into two categories - Fiction and Non-Fiction.
....

Fiction books are books with imaginary characters in which the author creates an entirely different world for the narrator; Fantasy, Science Fiction, Mystery, Horror, Romance, Historical Fiction, Dystopian, Young Adult, Adventure, Poetries, Mangas, and Comics fall under this category.

Alternatively,

Non-fiction books deal with real people, events, instructions, and information. Books like biographies, autobiographies, history, science, self-help, travel checklists, cookbooks, business, health, and exam guides fall under this category.

Once you finish dividing your books, deal with the lesser pile first. There are two types of people in this world. One who believes every fictional character is a real human being and one who treats stories like stories. I belong to the former category. As a result, my collection of nonfiction is comparatively less than the fictional ones.

When you deal with the non-fiction categories, remember their true purpose. The writer wrote it to provide information. Once you have learned the ideas and lessons you are supposed to, what good can you reap holding onto it?

For exam guides, study books, and references, donate them to a charity or at your local library. If you recently graduated, search for juniors who require that particular book. My mom would never let us keep old textbooks. Eventually, those

PRACTICAL TIPS THAT WILL HELP YOU DECLUTTER YOUR HOUSE

textbooks get used by my school juniors or the paper recycler.

Involving someone close who understands the true purpose of an item is a great way to maximize effective decision-making. If I stubbornly hold onto any textbook, she used to ask me, "How are you going to put that book into use?"

Her question often puzzled me and put me in deep thought, other than the vague answer that 'I might look up to it again.' There was no other excuse that I could make.

Once you deal with the lesser pile, you will be surprised that the amount almost vanishes. Hardly a countable book will be left, or no book at all.

Among the category of non-fiction books, cookbooks are tricky to part ways with as they often hold emotional values. One functional way I recommend is to keep the ones that contain unique recipes that are not readily available on the internet.

If there's a book with only one recipe that intrigues you, keep that recipe's information stored as a PDF or write it in your handy notebook and discard the rest.

When it comes to a fiction book, the best way to deal with it is by asking yourself if it is a story that you would love to switch roles with the main character.

It must always be the main character and never anybody else. Fictional side characters divert our attention from the main story and make us live the story as bystanders.

The book has been written primarily for the main characters, so if you cannot convince yourself to switch roles with the main characters, that book deserves to be set free for its authentic holders.

Applying this tactic will help you manage your home library and leave you with stories you adore. There are plenty of fictional characters that you will cross paths with, but only a few will leave a permanent mark on your life.

Another effective bookkeeping strategy I invented is keeping a limited amount by restricting myself from buying any new ones until I finish what's left to read in my collection.

I have informed all my friends about this decision, so every time I'm out hunting for new books or happen to find myself inside a bookstore, they remind me of my decision, and I instantly divert my attention. Since I refuse to believe that unread books will stay unread, I find this method quite practical for managing my unread collection.

Following this strategy will modify your outlook toward purchasing new books and also discipline you to cherish what you own. Choose books that make your home library a treasure trove for you.

If you can convince yourself to be at ease reading digital books, opt for PDFs or Kindle. Those digital versions of books are a cost-effective way to free up house library spaces.

Papers

Papers are one of the most disarranged items in our homes. No one can comprehend which specific paper will be of use or when. Since papers can range from rough notes to important documents, one must rely on critical thinking to deal with them. To start your paper tidying process, first divide them into the six following categories.

* **Category 1: Financial Documents**

Financial Documents are Bank Statements, Credit Card Statements, Mortgage or Lease Agreements, Investment Statements, Tax returns, Pay Stubs, Insurance Policies, Property Tax Bills, Utility Bills, Receipts, and Loan Documents.

* **Category 2: Household and Property**

Household and Property will contain Home Improvements, Contracts and Receipts, Home Inventory Records, Appliance Manuals, Home Warranty Information, Property Deeds and Titles, Rental Agreements, and HOA Documents.

* **Category 3: Personal and Legal Documents**

Personal and Legal Documents are Birth Certificates, Wills and Trusts, Power of Attorney Documents, Social Security Card Documents, Marriage Licenses, Passports, Driver Licenses, Adoption Papers, Divorce Decrees, and Military Records.

* **Category 4: Medical and Health Documents**

Medical and Health Documents are Insurance Cards, Immunization Records, Dental Records, Vision Care Records, Medical Bills, Prescription Records, and Health Insurance Policies.

* **Category 5: Children and Education**

The Children and Education section will have School Records, Report Cards, Vaccination Records, Extracurricular Activity Records, College Applications, and Financial Aid Documents.

* **Category 6: Miscellaneous**

Miscellaneous contains documents such as Receipts of Electronics, Magazines, Newspapers, Flyers, Warranties, Guarantees, Manuals, Coupons, and Sticky Notes.

Once you finish categorizing your papers into these six categories, start with the group containing the least number of items. If your child is in school or enrolled in academic classes, report cards, and certificates will hold more significant value than a parent whose children are busy parenting their own kids.

Decide the need of each category as per their urgency. Switch your mindset to functionality. If the paper falls under the daily use category, or if discarding the paper will put you in more trouble than ease, it is advisable to keep those vital papers.

Use files to store important documents. Covered box files with dividers are best for keeping all important papers in one place.

One of the precarious categories in this exhaustive list is medical reports. The degree of their usefulness cannot be comprehended, especially if you have someone in your home under constant critical care.

For medical reports, it is better to make a separate file with dividers and keep all of the members' medical reports in them. If you belong to a nuclear family, you may notice that only one or two people in your home possess the most medical records.

Think about its purpose and how it can serve you in the present or future. This way, you will only focus on keeping the essential papers.

For Magazines and Manuals, discard them once you finish reading. Magazines are like trends created to enjoy and relinquish. If you put too much thought, magazines could loop you in the cycle of feelings.

My dad has a habit of storing manuals. But, when a product refuses to work, he is the first to advise looking up on the internet or directly calling the technician. How did we tackle his manual collection habit? We discard every non-essential manual after a few months or a year, focusing on the product's functionality.

Komono

The term "Komono" in Japanese has a word list of its own. It is a vague word that includes every minor or significant thing your house contains.

Boxes of hairpins, rubber hair bands, cotton balls, articles, miscellaneous items, accessories, gadgets, small tools, parts of attachment, and all-encompassing things fall into the category of Komono.

The best way to sort this diverse section is by grouping them into broader categories such as:

- Pen drives & Flash drives
- Skin Care Products
- Makeup & Cosmetics
- Accessories
- Valuables like passports, credit cards, social security cards, loose change, etc.
- Digital cameras, appliances, electronics, cords, and unidentified parts of products.
- Household Supplies: Toilet papers, disposables, cleaning equipment, etc.
- Kitchen Kits: Kitchen goods, foil papers, plastic wraps, etc.

After grouping each item, think about its purpose, followed by the frequency at which you would need them. Current passports hold more value than expired ones. Choosing containers to store loose buttons is a hoarder's bait. Donate old buttons to your local tailor or sell them to a stationary shop for extra cash. If the spare button belongs to an expensive coat, sew it into the inner lining to keep it intact with the apparel.

For accessories, let go of any item that does not suit your current taste and style, or is rusted and damaged. Do the same with electrical products. Broken products are dead. Why do you want to hold onto a corpse that is desperate to be re-born? Discard and recycle every unidentified object.

Storing loose change at different places in your home will never make it out to the world. It will either rust or be forgotten if you decide to shift locations. Keep loose change in your pockets and purses so that it gets used. If you wish to save the money, choose to keep it in the bank. Treat it as a crucial resource.

Unless you refine your discarding ability and understand the true function of each item, sorting household supplies and kitchen kits can perplex your potential to think critically. The best examples of this category are toilet paper and kitchen wraps.

After the pandemic, these sets of items have become the most prized possession in every household. The fear of running out of necessities has haunted us so much that it is engraved in our hearts. The best way to overcome the trauma is by initially storing supplies for only 2 months.

If it's a cosmetic you use regularly, buying two packs is sufficient to support you for one and a half to two months. You can always restock once you are about to run out of the 2nd bottle. All products come with an expiry date. To make minimalistic, mindful purchases, understand how frequently you use the item and the product's shelf-life.

For Kitchen rolls, napkins, toilet paper, plastic wraps, and every single item used by your family members, a two-month supply is enough to support everyone's needs. Once you gradually overcome the fear of scarcity, invest in the required quantity for each month.

Electronic Packages of large products and electrical cords should be mindfully kept depending on your situation. My family often moves around the globe. As a result, my mother always stores cardboard boxes of large electrical items. The best way to store cardboard boxes is to keep them deflated. If you tear the sticky tape and unfold the corners, it will return to its original shape and then you can tie them in a bundle for future use.

Always store them in an accessible spot. As for essential cords, use large school or hiking bags to store them. Unlike labeling them in different boxes, bags with lots of pockets make cords handy.

My dad has a black hiking backpack where he stores the electrical cords. He has designated specific pockets for identical cords. Every time he is in need, all he does is command us which pocket to dig in and we discover the essential cord in minutes.

Items bought on a whim such as the latest health craze electronics, and free novelty goods are better to be discarded. Unless you are using the sticky pad with the label of a pharmaceutical company, and spending at least thirty minutes every day on the fat trimmer machine, they are pure junk for your household.

I understand you have spent your entire fortune on it. But keeping unused items hostage because it is expensive makes you feel more unproductive and incompetent. If the product is in good shape, you can always ask your local gym instructor to put it into use or sell it to someone in need.

If it is a gifted item, it would be better to look forward to the next sections ahead.

The Desperate Need To Hold Onto Disposables and Gifts

Disposables

Let me ask you a question. What do you mean by disposables? What is the true definition of it?

If you cannot answer the above question, here is the definition: Disposables are items designed to throw. Its synonyms are throw-away, expendable, one-use, and items that can be abandoned or destroyed after use.

The word disposable in itself means to dispose, not to keep. Saving those plastic spoons, take-out containers, straws, and boxes of every little item makes your house a trash bin. The seller is giving out those items with the idea that you will dispose of them immediately after use.

Why are you deliberately holding onto the trash of a different person? If you think those paper cups will be a convenient choice for family parties or picnics. You can easily purchase them depending on the number of attendees.

Another contributing factor to storing disposables is their ability to compel us to see them as a practical item in our household. Sticky notes and boxes of loose tissue convince us that we might need the items for future use.

When you find yourself trapped in throwing away disposables, stop and ask yourself, can it be swapped with more functional items, plastic straws can be exchanged with metal or pasta straws depending on the beverage's temperature.

If you are eating outside or order takeout at home do not bring or keep unused straws, tissues, and foil plates with the hope that they might come in handy for another use. Disposables are mostly made of non-biodegradable items, the more you let the thought of their importance influence you, the more you will produce junk not only in your household but also in the environment and your surroundings.

Gifts

Gifts are items given to a person without a payment. The only thing that the giver can expect from the gift taker is reciprocation of their warm feelings. Holding onto gifts with guilt that a person might get offended if you throw them away causes more dent in your relationship than actually throwing those gifts away.

The person who gave you the gift wants you to cherish it, use it, or keep it associated with your good thoughts. Nobody would willingly want to be on your stress list. Eliminate gifts that do not bring joy when you see and hold them or are dysfunctional.

When you hold onto items that weigh down your feelings, you unconsciously torment the shared bond. Utilize daily use gifts such as kitchen appliances, coffee mugs, photo frames, accessories, clothes, and bedding. Keeping them inside your closet for future use will only be counted as free clutter for your next cleaning session.

If it is an expensive decorative, ask yourself if it compliments your present home décor. Does that picture frame match your taste and style, if it does, decorate the piece or put the items into regular use.

Sometimes we tend to hoard heaps of expensive home decorations with the thought of using them in the future. Later those items only accumulate dust in the storerooms until they are non-functional enough to discard.

Sell the decorative if it's in good shape or donate it to someone whose house it can complement.

Letters and arts & crafts by children and dear ones fall under keepsakes, which we will discuss in the next chapter. But first, let go of every gift that does not add value to your present self.

Mementos

Mementos are the most difficult items to let go of, but have a profound payoff once you do.

Every item given by near and dear ones or created by you comes under mementos. People from large families often tend to send these tokens back home with the hope that they will retrieve them.

But the house where your parents live is not an empty closet to store your former emotions.

If you think about it rationally, the letters of your old boyfriends are a refined waste for your parents. It has been ages since you have moved out of that house. Why would you want to transform it into a haunted place of trash?

Dispose of every item that sparks the idea of sending it away to your parents. It has lived its purpose and does not serve your present self. When it comes to gifts by dear ones like greeting cards from a close relative, or arts and crafts by your children, think about its purpose.

If your children have grown up, ask them if they still remember the item that they made in kindergarten. You will be surprised to know that they would be the ones who would request you to discard those old gifts immediately.

If a greeting card holds valuable information like addresses or details of a particular relative, scan and save the information in a digital folder and let go of the physical one. Greeting cards are materialistic gestures to convey that the person associates you with their good thoughts.

When it comes to photographs and letters, give yourself a moment and analyze each one. Does that spark any euphoric feeling inside you? Do you feel the urge to share them with your people? Is it a picture you want to scan and save in your digital folder? If a photograph or letter does not motivate you to scan, save, or share it with another person. It is best to let go of that snapshot.

I discarded each of my friends' forgotten belongings that I received during high school. The only precious mementos that I own currently can easily be kept confined in a small handy thermocol container which I often unbox to relive those moments.

When you begin discarding items from the category of mementos and komono you will find astounding stockpiles of items you never knew existed in your home. Uncountable loose earbuds, crumpled paper foils, empty toilet rolls, damaged coils, expired package foods, unused medicines, over-the-counter expired drugs, spare papers, age-old prescriptions, outdated cosmetics, unidentified broken parts of old electronics, packets, and packets of batteries, broken watches, toothpicks and the list will keep increasing.

Don't let yourself sulk at the thought of 'just because' or 'just in case', rather take a firm decision whether to keep it or let it go.

If you feel frozen at making a decision, examine the item from a third person's perspective. Do you think somebody would willingly want to hold onto that item? If not, Throw it in an instant.

Another great way to de-freeze your decision-making capability is following the two Ds of Tidying.

The Two Ds of Tidying: Discard & Decide

Cleaning your house needs critical thinking. It often invites choice paralysis if we keep switching between the thought of items to discard and items to keep.

To truly make your house tidy, discard first and then decide. When I read this advice, I thought it was an absolute bluff, but when I implemented it, I tackled tons of clutter within six hours.

When you decide to declutter, your mind becomes ruthless. Every item that catches your attention gets analyzed with practicality. So, until your mind hints that you must keep an item, followed by a functional reason. Discard every item that you see.

When my mom begins her scheduled cleaning, she starts energized, paces down in the middle, and becomes an uncontrolled decluttering machine by the end. Since she has a lot of people to look after, she always has to clean within a specific period, for which her critical thinking ability always triggers when she is running out of time.

Everything she sees is clutter, possibly including us. This attitude of hers was the chief point for selling my books to the recycler, and the valid reason I shared in the above chapters that how would I put those used old textbooks into use was enough to silence me.

In the last years of your life, nobody will remember you for holding onto unnecessary items. They will remember the way you make them feel. So, keep only those items that serve you and make your living easy.

Once you clear out every item that does not add meaning to your present self, it is time to designate a proper place for each of them. Like you have a home to live in, your belongings deserve a space too.

Designate a specific spot for each category and make the regularly used items accessible to prevent playing hide and seek in times of need.

The Five Elements Approach

The Chinese term Feng Shui is a brilliant way to understand the essence of homes in our lives. The concept of Feng Shui originated in ancient China and claims to use forces to harmonize an individual with their surroundings. In easy terms, it is the study of finding correlations between humans and the universe.

The idea of Feng Shui is to incorporate the concept of the five elemental energies to bring balance to your life. It focuses on furniture placements, mirrors, plants, lighting, colors, water pathways, windows, decorative objects, artworks, doors, and passages.

If you focus specifically on the household items Feng Shui dwells around, you might purchase excessive products to re-design your indoors. The minimalistic approach to implementing Feng Shui in your home is through the symbolism of each element.

Below is a chart to help you get familiar with the energy of the five elements.

ELEMENT	SYMBOLISM
WOOD	Growth, Vitality, Flexibility
FIRE	Energy, Transformation, Passion
EARTH	Stability, Grounding, Nurturing
METAL	Clarity, Focus, Order
WATER	Flow, Adaptability, Purification

Understanding this chart is essential because it will further nurture your inner minimalist. Feng Shui emphasizes keeping a clean, organized space with an adequate quantity of furniture, lighting, and plants to maintain the flow of elemental energy in your home.

When we do not put conscious effort into arranging and designating a place for each item we block the energy flow in our homes.

To take it a step further, categorize each item of your home into five groups of elements. Here's how you can incorporate the idea of Feng Shui for each category in your home.

Wood

The element Wood symbolizes growth, vitality, and flexibility.

Household items like sturdy wooden wall cabinets with shelves, multi-purpose wardrobes like closets with hidden spaces, and smart foldable beds are best to incorporate in this section.

Keep key furniture of your home like your bed, desk, and couch in a commanding position where you can easily see the door without being directly in line with it. This specific placement of the home furniture creates a sense of security and control over your life.

Invest in only necessary quality pieces of furniture. Saving a few bucks and choosing flimsy, fancy items will fill your home with trash much quicker than expected. **Fancy**

things that are not functional become undisposed waste once the luster fades. It is better to invest in multifunctional items that can benefit not only you but also your future generations.

I have a wooden bed in my home that belongs to my grandma. She bought it when she married my grandfather, and later, I received it from her. Both of them are deceased now, but the bed is still intact even after my dog chewed off the sides of its headboard.

Why? Because the headboards could be disassembled, it was easy for my dad to change the damaged parts for me. It also has a big cabinet where you can store bedding, which makes it a keepsake for my mom.

Another item included in wood is bookshelves. Bookshelves add interest to your decor. If you own a spacious area, use bookshelves as wall dividers. Bookshelves with cabinets will help you store more valuable belongings than a box with a few shelves.

Swap small kitchen utensils such as spoons, ladles, and chopsticks into wooden ones. Only buy as per the needs of your family. If you belong to a nuclear family, having twenty sets of spoons and fifteen sets of identical plates is just accumulated junk in your kitchen.

Fire

The element Fire symbolizes Energy, Transformation, and Passion. Items like the choice of lighting in your room fall under this category. I have read and seen a hundred reels that emphasize having dim or warm lights that mimic the cycle of the Sun. I appreciate the idea but do not recommend it while cleaning.

Bright lights make me feel more energized and productive than having a soft radiance in my room.

I prefer to live in extremes, so if I don't want lights, then it is absolute darkness. There's no in-between. In my aunt's room, she used to have two lights, and she always switched on the dim light during the evening, which made the room look sick, according to my perspective. So, when I dealt with the clutter in her room, I always switched on the bright lights.

Bright lights create a sense of urgency and keep you alerted. It makes you more productive at tackling tasks. Once you finish cleaning, you can always choose the idea of mimicking the Sun's cycle, but when you clean a specific area of your house, make sure to light up the space properly.

The best example to help you understand the importance of bright lights is Hospitals. Have you ever seen a patient waiting area, administration counter, or pharmacy using dim lights? Think about it!

As per the idea of Feng Shui, the ideal lights for a home during easy hours are natural lights, and a balance of adequate and warm lighting helps to flow yang (positive) energy indoors.

Earth

Earth symbolizes Stability, Grounding, and Nurturing. Even though the items in the element wood are counted on Earth and vice versa. I prefer to associate this element with plants only.

Plants nurture our environment. It makes the world thrive. Without plants, the entire population would be wiped out from this planet. Similarly, to make your home inviting, you can choose low-maintenance indoor plants.

Plants need constant care, for which many working individuals prefer to exclude them from their home setting. But if you opt for indoor plants like bamboo, snake plants, peace lilies, cast iron, spider plants, etc. The quality of your indoor air will improve drastically. Indoor plants can survive on negligence. It purifies harmful toxins like benzene, formaldehyde, and xylene and keeps in-house air clean.

If your home has large windows or spaces where sunlight peeks in, keep the plants near those spaces. People who prefer living in compact compartments and students living in dormitories can easily choose small indoor plants that they can keep on study tables or shelves.

I found the true potential of indoor plants during a house shift. We recently moved to a new place, and my mom had yet to assign her plants a designated spot. It was late, so we did not bother to separate outdoor plants from indoor ones and left all of them in the living room.

The following day, I was surprised by how inviting the space looked. Even if we had recently shifted and the whole house was dusty and uncleaned, the ambiance of that space felt refreshing. It made me stay around the living room the entire day until the plants were out again.

According to the idea of Feng Shui, plants represent life and growth that enhances the flow of positive energy in our surroundings. However, dead and wilting plants are believed to drain out the positive energy from your home. When you choose plants for your indoors, invest in one or a few plants first and be very mindful while tendering them.

Metal

Humans discovered metals out of sheer luck. Through the discovery of fire, we learned that metals are malleable, and according to our needs and wants, we could shape them. It symbolizes clarity, focus, and order. Our houses are homes to an array of metals. Metals make our lives more convenient. Holding onto items that do not serve you in any manner is a waste of resources.

Items like organizer kits, multifunctional tools, and smart devices fall under this category. The true purpose of metal is to establish order in our homes. When buying home decor, switch to your minimalist mindset and only choose those items that bring clarity and order to your homes and yourself.

The best example of this item is vintage-style nail cutters. If you examine 90's nail cutters, you will realize that a single tool can host your entire spa day. It comes with a nail file, dirt remover, cutter, and several other tools whose names I don't yet know, all while being compact enough to carry in your pockets. I have never upgraded my taste when it comes to nail cutters. Those 90's nail cutters are one of my prized possessions.

The concept of Feng Shui often promotes oval and circular shapes of metals more than the other shapes. The round shape represents the cyclical nature of life and completeness. Offices, study areas, and other workspaces that demand organization and productivity can benefit from the energy the element metal brings. Choose metallic door frames, metallic round framed mirrors, wall colors, and metallic light fixtures over regular ones.

Water

Water symbolizes flow, adaptability, and purification. To incorporate the energy of water in making our living spaces effective, one should focus on deep cleaning.

My mom has a habit of mopping the floors every day. In contrast, my aunt can hardly convince herself to clean her floors once every two weeks. But even with different cleaning patterns, none of the houses seems untidy at one glance. The reason is floors. The floors of your house decide how often you need to deep clean.

Houses with toddlers and pets need to be more hygienic and clean than a house with working adults. The best way to effectively keep spaces squeaky clean is by utilizing cleaning equipment and solutions. Choose effective manufactured bathroom cleaning products over homemade DIYs. Prolonged periods of using DIY techniques and products leave a yellow stain on the tiles.

Home decor like carpets and thick rugs should be washed thoroughly once every two to three months, depending on the frequency of its use. You can easily opt for dry washing certain items depending on the material. Harpic bombs in toilet tanks can keep your toilets sparkling for months.

When it comes to incorporating the theory of Feng Shui, water could be tricky to implement as it is believed that flowing water symbolizes the continuous flow of positive energy and wealth. It emphasizes the idea of keeping aquariums and water fountains which often contradicts the idea of a minimalistic mindset.

Artworks and mirrors also possess great value in the ideology of Feng Shui. However, these decorative items also often contradict the idea of minimalism and mindful purchases. If you wish to incorporate items such as mirrors and artwork in your room décor, focus on the quantity. One full mirror and one compact mirror are enough to cater to both your makeup and costume check.

Do not directly place the mirror, opposite the front door. In Feng Shui, it is believed that the reflective surfaces of mirrors can bounce out positive energy from your home.

They act as an amplifier of energies, placing them thoughtfully to brighten dark areas of your house will symbolically increase vitality and positivity.

If you are choosing to invest in artwork, focus on the energy you want to invite in that particular space of your house. Lively, bright-colored artworks symbolize vibrant energy and should be kept in areas like the living room, and other social places in your home. For bedrooms and relaxation areas, opt for calming images to create a sense of peacefulness during low rush hours.

Avoid or use fewer paintings and artworks that evoke sadness, loneliness, and bitterness. Art pieces that create a strong sense of uneasiness make house spaces alarming. Choose a place for each of your artwork strategically.

Doors and Pathways are considered as a prime source of allowing Chi in your household. The main entrance of your home is considered to be the mouth of Chi, so it is recommended to keep the main door spaces clean, well-lit, and organized. Keep fewer items to not hinder the flow of energy into your home. Doors that open without any obstruction symbolize welcoming positive energy and new opportunities.

On the other hand, windows are considered to bring positive energy into our homes, through the help of air. Glass windows should be regularly scrubbed and polished. Lighter materials of curtains are preferred to allow the flow of yang energy into our homes.

If you ever find yourself puzzled about implementing these five elemental approaches in cleaning or organizing your space, refer to the symbolism of each element. The true purpose of this technique is to create a holistic environment for your living.

Surprise yourself by inventing your elemental list.

CHAPTER 4:
THE REAL GOAL IS NOT TO CLEAN THE HOUSE BUT...

How often did you find yourself greeted by clutter within a few weeks after you finished your mini-marathon of cleaning? Quite often?

Rebound will keep re-entering your premises if you do not understand the true goal of cleaning.

Imagine you finally summon the energy to clean up your entire room, wipe off each speck of dust, and get rid of every dish in the sink. You find your mind replaying the productive moment repeatedly until a week passes and a new pile of waste is waiting for you to tackle.

Every person who has taken the initiative to clean has faced multiple rounds of rebound. Waste rebound cannot subside if you do not fix your habits. You can make cleaning an event and declutter your entire house in a day. But if you return to the attitude of a procasticlutter, trash will eventually resurge.

To ward off rebound from your house premises, focus on building small habits like the ones we discussed at the end of Chapter 1 and up till now.

Focus on keeping items where they belong; by developing small habits of doing dishes right after you eat or folding the clothes right after the laundry, you will soon start noticing that not every hour of the day feels rushed. Following these small habits will prevent your home from looking like a theft scene and also free up time from your schedule.

Involve your family and assign them effortless tasks like filling water bottles, keeping the item where it belongs after using it, making their bed, sorting the letters before stacking them, emptying the trash bin before it gets filled, and so on.

The real goal is not to clean the house but to keep the house clean. I will repeat. **The real goal is not to clean the house but to keep the house clean.** It is not about waiting for clutter to accumulate but about changing the habits that lead to the heap.

You can tidy your whole house in a day or two, regardless of the dimensions of your home. But if you keep following the same old habits, the goal of a spotless home will always be out of your reach.

In the following pages, I will share six ideas to help you tackle old clutter, identify functional items for your home, keep the tidying ball rolling, and begin your minimalistic journey.

Task or Treasure

Author Marie Kondo was the first to make me realize that tidying is a one-day event. I appreciated the idea, but I disagreed. I have valid **REASONS** for it.

The house I currently live in is surrounded by canopies of trees and a substantial backyard where you might find garden fairies if you believe. Nevertheless, creatures that people dislike make homes in my abode. Cocoons on walls and spider nets on window grills are our primary house decorations. Note the sarcasm.

Adding to this list my furry friends and every single pet I have in my house makes it a mini zoo that needs maintenance every three to six months. Having a lot of items to deal with slows down the cleaning process, and tidying the entire house in a day is next to impossible. But we cannot let the fear of waste prevent us from living.

The best way to deal with old accumulated waste is to assign yourself a deadline of two days. Prepare every possible item that has the potential to be of use during cleaning and have a person to hold yourself accountable for.

Ask your roommate, family member, or best friend to be your private bank for a day and deposit a significant amount to them. Make sure it is someone whom you can genuinely trust.

If trusting others is difficult, you can deposit the money in your other bank account or somewhere safe in your home, for example, your wallet.

Once you deposit, send or keep the money. Now, invest an entire day discarding every non-functional item from your home. Money holds the utmost importance in every individual's life. You cannot survive if you don't have money for your necessities. So, keeping a considerable amount of money at stake that would impact your life is a great way to hold yourself accountable for your laziness.

When you put something precious at stake, the want to clean your home becomes a desperate need. This technique is best for people who struggle to begin their cleaning journey because of the overwhelming heap of accumulated junk. The fear of losing the entire amount only because you failed to make a significant change provides the right amount of dopamine to trigger critical thinking.

On Day 1, Be ruthless and discard everything that is not functional, un-serving, or does not spark tremendous joy. Constantly remind yourself what you risked to keep yourself on track. By the end of the day, you will realize that you have disposed of every insignificant item from your home. Once you finish, you can start deep cleaning the dust.

On Day 2, Focus on arranging the items and doing your routine household chores. Designate a specific spot for each valuable item, and return every item where it belongs after use.

I advise people to designate two days to clean their house because if you keep deciding on a specific space for the valuable items while you discard the unnecessary, you will soon find yourself drained and unmotivated. Our mind gets tired when we constantly switch between ideas. The brain becomes puzzled at identifying and analyzing if an item is a task to deal with or a treasure to keep.

Always think of the functionality and value of an item when you discard it. Consider the frequency of using an item and keep it in an accessible place when choosing a designated spot for the items you are keeping. Assigning two consecutive days will keep you energetic and refine your decision-making ability.

If you succeed, you can choose to spend or save the money for yourself. If you fail to make significant progress within two days, donate it or ask your friend or family member to use the entire amount for themselves.

I first tried this technique, when my friends from junior school planned to have a get-together at my home. The initial plan was only to have a small gathering and return to each other respective houses, but considering the sudden stretch of hours in house parties, two of my close friends decided to stay for the night.

If I were still a packrat, I wouldn't have bothered having a messy room, but I was changed so I decided to clean the entire house in a day, even places they never knew existed in my new home. In the process, I found myself completely drained when it was time to clean my room. I started my cleaning process in the morning and by night, there were still areas that needed my attention.

The constant arranging and rearranging of the items made me feel so unproductive that I gave up midway. When my friends visited, they complimented me for the change in surroundings but I could not convince myself that I genuinely made significant progress.

A week later, the same friend called me and asked me to help her arrange the bookshelf that she shared with her brother and I decided to take the initiative to make myself productive. However, on the day of cleaning her bookshelf, I reached her home quite late due to traffic and the uncountable number of study and reference books she owned was far greater than what I expected.

Only sorting the items as per her brothers and her needs consumed our entire evening. So, we decided to arrange the bookshelves the next day once the courier dropped her new book collection.

The next day when we arranged the items after the courier arrived, it hardly took us 15 minutes to color-coordinate her fiction books as per her taste. There was no fatigue in arranging and rearranging the same books again and again as per the thickness or width to make it look ordered and balanced. We freed up two entire shelves which even her new book collection could not devour.

Make Your House Force You to Greet

Let's say you are waiting for your train on an uncrowded subway. You can easily spot the faces of the people surrounding you, and your eyes catch the sight of a person standing near the station clock. Before you can avert your eyes, you realize that the person is wearing clothes of your taste. Something that you would recommend or compliment upon.

You resist looking in their direction, but the more you steal glances, the more intrigued you get. You try to divert your attention from their striking features, but they move closer to your spot, and you notice little nuances of them that make you smile.

The thought of knowing their name crosses your mind, but you distract yourself by checking the time. You become self-conscious and quickly check your appearance, fixing your hair, trying to look oblivious. Your mind tells you to say hello, but you feel frozen at your feet. The person has a similar habit of tapping their fingers as they play a song on repeat.

You could hear the faint sound of music from their headphones and realize it's your favorite song. A song that you never thought anybody would listen to. A song that you often listen to when you seek comfort. Your heart starts to beat faster as you decide to introduce yourself.

But the moment you speak, they start to brag about themselves.

Do you think you would love to know more about that person? Would you willingly re-greet yourself? Nobody wants to deal with a snob. A person with excessive pride over futile achievements could never contribute significantly to another person's life.

Our homes are similar to humans. Just like every person has a personality, our houses have theirs. The things you choose to decorate your house with become their prized possession. Why do you want your house to have a terrible impression? Houses are built to provide comfort, protection, and security from the chaos of the outside world. In return, they only expect us to value their presence.

A clean house looks inviting and calm. A cluttered house creates anxiety and stress. If your house were a person, would you want it to provide tension?

The architecture of your house reflects your style, and the interior of your house conveys your ideal mood. The clutter that you keep avoiding can narrate stories of your traits. Build a home that welcomes you wholeheartedly after a tiring day. A home that adds meaning to your life. A house that shares unforgettable stories. A home that convinces you to greet it with a smile.

Refrain from Passing Your Clutter Burden

If you have ever cleaned your house while living with siblings, best friends, or family, you might have caught yourself donating items to them that you do not need.

A new coffee mug that you got as a freebie. A cute little summer dress that you have outgrown but your sister would fit in. Earrings that were brought on a whim and do not complement your face shape, a new T-shirt that you picked but never happened to wear.

Donating items to your family members with the hope that they might put them to use is a common practice in every household.

Younger siblings and parents are most susceptible to these kinds of donations.

But think about it consciously. Does that dress reflect your sister's taste in clothing? Does that T-shirt material make your dad feel comfortable?

If you ask them directly, they will happily give you a pleasing answer but later stress about finding new places to keep that refined clutter. I used to receive clothes from an elder sister of mine. Her mother always took extra care of her dresses, and as a family ritual, when I obtained it, I found it brand new.

I used to love receiving those clothes and wore them often. But as I grew up, my style varied from hers. We stopped sharing clothes, but when I took the initiative to clean my closet, I found a heap of old clothes that did not suit my current taste. I spent hours procrastinating about what I would say if her mother questioned me about those clothes.

Since we both had outgrown those clothes, there was no point in re-exchanging them. We did not even know any person who had the potential to fit in those clothes. So, we settled matters by deciding to throw them all away, but before we could, my mother jumped in and said she would put them into use.

Arguing with mothers is futile, so we let her keep them, and after a few days, I found them again in my closet. When I asked my mother, she gave a valid excuse that she could not find any other place to keep them.

Those dresses again revolved in my home, causing hindrance to my organizational skills. When I decided to step down to owning a small collection of clothes, I invested in a small wardrobe that had three broad shelves, two covered drawers, three small glass-cased sections, and an open shelf where I could easily showcase my book collection.

The entire set could hold my clothes, books, gifts, files, papers, and cosmetics. I felt proud of my purchase. It was one of the first multifunctional items I had bought for myself, but those extra clothes wreaked havoc in my closet. Even if I could fit all the clothes using the newly learned folding techniques, making peace with it was tough.

I could not blame my mother, nor could I blame my sister for giving me those clothes. I brooded over my inefficiency, but before it could consume me, my family shifted locations. In the process, I accidentally mistook the package for another one, and we left it at our old address.

I realized I had forgotten to pick up that package as soon as we moved into our new home. But the freedom it brought discarding those items was more profound than the guilt of being irresponsible.

Burdening your family and peers with your clutter is never a good decision. Gift things that hold value, not things that will soon be out of use. The moment you decide to make your family go through your bags of clutter, the very moment you re-invite rebound in your home.

Stop shifting your stuff in the name of discarding, have an honest conversation about the need for the item with the person you thought giving it to, and break the generational trauma of burdening clutter.

You Only Need 7 Sets of Loungewear

Downgrading to 7 Sets of loungewear might feel daunting initially. But with practice, you will be able to have a closet that can support you for six months at least.

My family always downgrades outerwear into home clothes, especially my mother. She could easily don every outerwear at home regardless of the material. On the contrary, I even struggle to wear full sleeves at home.

As soon as I step into my house, I instantly change into my oversized T-shirt and shorts. It has become such an irresistible habit that sometimes I get surprised by how unconsciously and quickly I change into my home clothes.

For me, comfort is crucial, and no matter how much people argue that you should wear fancy clothes at home to shift your mindset or feel good about yourself.

The sheer relief that loose cotton T-shirts give is incomprehensible. I never downgrade my outerwear to my home clothes, not even inners. Clothes meant to be styled as outerwear or created to make you look fancy can hardly provide comfort at home.

Refrain from downgrading outerwear into home clothes. It will make your purchases mindful and help you understand how many clothes are enough to serve you in different weathers.

The first time I decided to own seven sets of loungewear was when I got intrigued by the idea of building a rainbow closet. Although I prefer to wear neutral colors outside, a few Instagram reels influenced me about colors and color theory.

So, I decided to wear mono-tone cotton shorts and T-shirts at home. To abstain from decision paralysis, I chose the seven focal colors of a rainbow.

The best part about the impulsive decision to make myself look like cotton candies was I could mix and match the colors and create a whole new outfit. It has been more than six months since I purchased my home clothes. The set and material I invested in are enough to support and comfort me the entire summer, spring, autumn, and the first half of winter.

Experimenting with home outfits helps you modify your perspective towards purchasing clothes. Our home outfits often surpass the number of clothes we style outside. The sudden shift of having only the necessary makes you cherish what you own. Soon, you will also be able to determine the amount of outerwear you need

One of the finest methods to start building a minimalist wardrobe is determining the clothing style and colors you prefer most. Some people choose jeans over shorts. Some prefer different shades of neutral colors over bright ones.

The apparel and colors that you opt less to wear are the items you need to stop investing in.

Another great method to analyze your needs regarding outerwear is taking the Project 333 challenge. Project 333 is a minimalist wardrobe challenge that encourages people to style only 33 items or less for three months. The 33 items must include pieces of jewelry, clothing, accessories, coats, jackets, and shoes.

Underwear, inners, and sentimental items like wedding rings are excluded from the 33-item list.

Go through your current wardrobe and pick thirty-three items considering your lifestyle, climate, and personal taste. Then plan your outfits for the upcoming three months without making any single purchase. At the end of the first 3 months, reflect on your entire style journey and analyze the differences in your perspective.

Here is a basic chart to help you get familiar with the number of items each apparel could consist of.

Tops, Jackets, Cardigans, Blazers, Sweaters, Hoodies, Buttoned Shirts, and T-shirts combinedly should consist of ten items or less.

Bottoms like jeans, trousers, shorts, joggers, skirts, and dress pants will only consist of six items or less.

When it comes to fancy dresses the number should be maintained to three or less.

Outerwear like trench coats, wool coats, and puffer jackets should consist of three items or less focusing on the thickness of each material to support you during changing weather.

Only 5 types of shoes including sneakers, boots, heels, flats, sandals, and loafers should be selected depending on the needs of the individual's lifestyle.

Essential accessories like scarves, belts, sunglasses, crossbody bags, watches, and minimalistic jewelry that can be paired in a versatile way should be picked.

The basic idea of selecting these 33 items is to mix and match outfits for different occasions while focusing on timeless pieces to build a capsule wardrobe that eliminates excessive purchasing.

This styling method was first introduced by Courtney Carver, who wrote a blog and styled 33 items of clothing in her office every day. Nobody seemed to notice it at first but later it became one of the effective ways to begin your minimalistic fashion challenge.

Make sure to pack the rest of the items and keep them out of sight. Once the 3 months are up styling those 33 items, you can choose to adjust your style as per the season preference.

The Project 333 challenge that proves less is far more is not only considered a fashion challenge but a key to exploring minimalism in your daily life. It simplifies decision-making, increases awareness, promotes less clutter, and enhances financial savings.

What You Own Must Serve You

While choosing clothes or keeping things you dearly love, focus on the purpose of every item. If the item cannot add sincere meaning to your life or make your life easy, let it go.

Thinking constantly about functionality will leave you with the exact quantity of items you should retain to feel content.

Even after discarding heaps of unwanted items, you might find yourself holding onto a specific amount of item that daunts you to keep. One such category is diaries for me. I have always been confused about determining the purpose and functionality of unused diaries.

I have a habit of penning thoughts in notebooks. So, since childhood, I always asked Dad to give me a diary from his office collection. By the time I grew up, Dad made it a habit of passing down each diary he saw.

As an outcome, I owned tons of unused diaries from the same year and previous years. Some are so old that the pages have become discolored. When I discarded my unwanted books and papers, I could not decide to throw them away since the frequency of their use was regular.

Although the number of unused diaries was higher than used ones, letting them go seems like a substandard choice. So, I held onto it unrelentingly until the thought that I might die before I could finish writing in them struck my mind.

I kept pondering on that single thought. The fear of missing out consumed me, and I started disliking receiving diaries from my father. I switched to penning thoughts digitally, but never in those diaries.

After a considerable amount of time, I confronted my father to stop gifting diaries to me, and he did. But suddenly, I found the urge to write on them again. The quantity of the diaries stopped bothering me all of a sudden.

I wrote in them quotidianly, and when I finished one, I donated it to the recycler. This cycle of completing one diary and donating it to the recycler became an earnest habit. Gradually, I found the pile of diaries manageable, and that's when it clicked that what I own must serve me in every possible way.

When you have already reaped the benefits of your favorite item, there is no point in keeping them around.

The happiness, joy, and comfort your favorite household item needs to provide to you has already played its part. Let go of it before it starts to count as waste. What you own must serve your present self.

The Surprising Effect of Taking a Pre-lunch and Pre-dinner Break

When I was a packrat before my breakthrough at my aunt's house, my mother always scolded me to help her with household work. Being the eldest child, I had already completed my years of domestic drudgery, so when my brother entered his teenage years, it was his turn to carry on the tradition.

Unfortunately, since he happened to be born under the lucky stars and ten years younger than me, my family played their affectionate card and kept me assigned to the dreadful work.

I used to be bothered, but after spending my days at my aunt's house, cleaning had become my favorite pastime. So, whenever I felt I needed a break, I cleaned the house. Since my mother was always so obsessive about keeping the house tidy, all I needed to complete was trivial household work, like filling up the water bottles, keeping the misplaced objects in their designated place, dusting my bookshelves, and organizing my closet, which hardly took a few minutes to complete.

But during weekends, I often find myself cleaning the same area or category of clutter I cleaned in the morning or the day before. It took time to realize that I was wasting my time on household chores rather than working or resting in my spare time. So, I decided to set a specific day to organize each area of my home.

I was sure I would be able to tackle the entire mess within a day since I had become quite efficient using timers and all the techniques that I have mentioned in this book.

But after spending an entire Sunday cleaning the disorganized spaces and my shared bookshelf. I saw my brother disarranging my ordered bookshelves to take out his textbooks and subconsciously misplacing items while in a rush.

Nevertheless, I arranged my bookshelves quotidianly once he left for school. But as soon as he returned, he put his books above mine, causing me to reorganize the bookshelves day and night.

Switching professions from clinical to writing made me understand that the time I could delegate to do the household chores has shortened.

When you work for a 9 to 5 job, you are expected to put a certain number of hours into it. Once you return home, you can choose to deal with the office work later.

But working from home, especially on projects you love, can hinder the attention of other sectors of your life. My concentration deteriorated when I chose to clean before working and If I wrote before cleaning, my thoughts revolved around tidying the disorganized places. It was an unending race that I tried to maintain pace with, but the amount of clutter never subsided.

The following Thursday, I took a short mid-day break and organized my bookshelf out of boredom. The next day, I repeated the same for some extra household chores. After a week, I noticed a difference in the amount of clutter built during the weekend. It was significantly less, and the places I had organized in the morning did not need any reorganizing in the evening.

That is when I realized taking a short pre-lunch and pre-dinner break to return every misplaced item to its designated spot has become a contributing factor in reducing my tidying load.

When you stay indoors, the items of your home are in constant use. As a result, we subconsciously misplace items when we are distracted or under rush hour. If you think carefully, weekends multiply the amount of waste from regular days.

I started this method especially to escape my weariness and keep my mom happy regarding cleaning. In contrast, I reduced my own tidying time effectively. This method is one of my little ways to keep the cleaning ball rolling. Taking a quick 5 to 10 minutes cleaning break will reset your mind and keep your house in order.

Do not dwell on time-consuming tasks. Focus on trivial errands like filling empty water bottles, arranging your work shelf, and organizing your daily wear to make your tidying effort count. Once the ten minutes are up, return to your work again.

You will be surprised by the effect of this pre-lunch and pre-dinner break and how it can reduce your tidying load effectively by the end of the day. After all, it is always the trivial tasks that accumulate and make cleaning a dire chore.

CHAPTER 5:
HOW AND WHY IT IS IMPORTANT TO LET GO OF UNNEEDED KEEPSAKES

The Joy of Being Surrounded by Things You Love

When I was six, I had a dress beaded with pearls and rhinestones. The dress made me feel like a princess from a Barbie series. I often wore it with my silver crown and pretended to be a magical princess hiding from a wicked witch.

When I was ten, I could not fit into that dress and started to use my mother's wardrobe collection to pretend to be a star kid who wanted to finish school without drawing attention.

She owned a beautiful black dress that sparkled whenever someone flashed a light over it. It was so pretty that I refused to return it to her and kept it with me.

But then I grew up, and those beautiful dresses were kept confined in my memento box. I did style my mother's dress, but it eventually wore off due to regular use, and I discarded it.

But that princess's dress was always with me. At every phase of life, I find myself peeking into that box and reminiscing about the lost time.

Every time things in my life went south, I found myself reopening the box to relive those moments. In the process, I never realized that it has become an escape mechanism to not deal with difficult situations or responsibilities.

I complained continuously about how I wished to be a kid again. I never really looked inside that box when I was happy. It was always those cruel times that forced me to hold onto that dress and sob.

When my mother offered to donate it, I refused. I could not make peace with the idea of discarding the dress. This conversation created a strife between us. She could not watch her daughter hugging a dress to weep rather than choosing to be a responsible kid. I could not believe the present was more beautiful than my past.

Amidst these periodic strifes, my mom donated the dress without informing me when I moved out of the house. When I returned, I hardly remembered that dress until I was arranging my sea shells, and the memento box seemed to have more space than usual. It took me an entire minute to understand what was missing, and when I realized I was more shocked about my delayed response than her donating the cloth.

When we choose our keepsakes, we often forget to focus on the functionality as it serves us significantly in terms of emotions. But as you keep holding onto items based on emotions, you will realize that you often find it arduous to channel those feelings.

You limit your growth and keep yourself from being in the present moment. Try to identify the feelings associated with each of your keepsakes. If the keepsake belongs to a tethered bond, there is no point in holding onto it just because you miss those happy memories with the person. Invest in the keepsakes that make you appreciate your present self, not something that urges you to own a time shuttle.

There is a difference between a box of dead dreams and dreams that inspire you to become your better self. I only have a box of seashells that reminds me to avoid burnout and visit the sea periodically, two small diaries that contain all the poems I have written till now, 25 non-identical pictures of my favorite people who urge me to dream more, and 27 books that inspire me to write better stories.

The pictures and books come in recyclable items. Once the color fades, or I don't find the book contributing enough, I will donate or discard them. The box of sea shells also gets recycled once or twice a year. The only non-recyclable items on this list are my two small diaries that might stay around, irrespective of the frequent house shifts.

Figure out what keepsakes celebrate your present self and only surround yourself with items that create veracious joy in you.

The Downside of Decluttering and Minimalism

Decluttering and Minimalism isolate you from the crowd of impulsive consumers. You will no longer stand in the sale queue or fight a fellow purchaser to secure the latest items on limited-time deals.

The idea of the American dream emerged because of the affluent opportunities the United States provided for every person. Author James Truslow Adams coined this term in his best-selling book Epic of America portraying a land that offers equal opportunities according to one's ability to lead an abundant life.

As society advanced, every article, newspaper, digital advertisement, and billboard filled us with the idea of consumerism and attaining perfectionism through aesthetics.

Have you ever bought an item on a salesperson's recommendation and later found out that it never really served you in any way?

Minimalism breaks the consumerist mindset and helps you identify the three essential resources of life. You will no longer find yourself purchasing on a whim or living paycheck after paycheck. It will help you understand what you truly need to thrive in this world and how chasing materialistic goals can never make you feel fulfilled.

It is true that without money, you cannot buy happiness, but spending too much money on quick dopamine will eventually make you sulk into exorbitant cortisol.

Take a day to examine your genuine needs. The items that make you happy for an extended period, things that you want others to remember you for. You will be surprised to see that hardly a handful of material things or none at all create an authentic sense of happiness and contentment inside you.

Minimalism and Decluttering will change your perspective of abundance. It helps you identify the real opportunities and makes you a magnet of good fortune.

CHAPTER 6:
THE GIFTS OF MINIMALISM & DECLUTTERING

Many studies, books, and documentaries explore and validate the link between minimalism and decluttering to enhance your overall being. When you declutter and shift your perspective from possession to abundance, you claim the three essential resources of life. TIME, MONEY, and HEALTH.

You create an environment that fosters your growth and individualism. It helps you identify and channel your true intentions to build a prosperous life. It sets an example for your future generation, releases unnecessary emotional baggage, and promotes mindful living, saving your time and energy for meaningful endeavors.

Here is a scenario that will help you have an in-depth idea of how having a minimalistic mindset transforms your being.

Scenario:

You own a house with every imaginable and unimaginable item you ever desired. It has libraries, a porch with cushioned swings, a perfectly tailored walk-in wardrobe, a golf space, and a spacious living room with color-coordinated couches.

You spent a fortune building your dream home and decorating it with every item that complimented your taste and style. But then you saw a magazine advertisement about equipping your house with the latest gadgets.

You renovate your home with the budget you secured from a new project and feel content. Soon, you find an email in your inbox that claims your gadgets are outdated.

At first, you did not care, but shortly, the home gadgets started malfunctioning, locking you out of your house. You ask for help and get introduced to better gadgets that cost you a loan but claim to be efficient enough to provide shelter in your home.

You took the loan out of necessity, and later, when you worked day and night to clear the EMIs, you saw your friends taking the forgotten trip, which you always insisted upon. You were short on cash, so you decided to skip the trip but later dwell on the missed opportunity and buy new items to compensate for the contentment.

Let us assume you did take the trip by asking your other friend to pitch in. But once you return, the EMIs and debt loom large over you. You sacrificed your sleep to work and pay off the loans. In the process, your health deteriorated, so you invested in a medical loan to treat your health.

In both situations, stress never left.

Now Imagine a home equipped with all your necessities. You only buy needed items that contribute to cleaner surroundings and more mental well-being. So, you spend your free time learning a new skill or talking to your family.

There's no monetary stress in your life, no EMIs to pay, no debts to clear. As you return from work, an inviting ambiance that does not demand immediate attention waits for you each day.

With less futile worries, you decide to utilize the leaves in your work bucket and plan a trip with friends. The discipline built at home radiates in the trip, garnering valuable attention from people who align with your goals and interests.

You appear influential and secure another business deal, establishing a new source that helps you earn more.

Which situation did you think made you feel content in terms of money, health, and time?

Minimalism does not mean earning less. It is about investing in materials and feelings that make your life worthwhile. It prevents you from making pointless decisions and gifts you a life imbued with intentions.

How Minimalism & Decluttering Will Make You a Magnet of Good Fortune

Decluttering and Minimalism create a ripple effect that positively influences various aspects of your life. As children, we associate our emotions with people who make us happy and content. But after growing up, we often shift our perspective to gaining materialistic items to seek the same comfort.

Buying item after item to validate our own emotions to ourselves will never make us feel content. Each product and advertisement that has been created gives us a false sense of entirety to fill a void in our lives. But the truth often hides under the pseudo words of the salesperson, the truth that no product in this world can provide us the feeling of having a whole life.

A minimalistic perspective helps you escape the network of consumerism and makes you understand less is more. It establishes your perspective of enough, setting you apart from the rat race of impulsive purchasers.

When you choose to declutter you not only honor your past but also make room for the new. Clean organized spaces promote mental clarity and prevent decision fatigue. You will no longer find yourself decorating your space with meaningless items. Each product that you purchase will have a practical reason followed by an intention to use.

It explores the idea of eradicating the excessive want of humans to purchase every item they are introduced to. The fact that not every purchase we are drawn to is needed for our survival can be attained through a minimalistic mindset.

The crowd will always get multiplied in the wish list of marketing diaries. What you want for your survival can only be identified through your own needs. No other individual can guarantee which item is essential to live your perspective of abundance.

Minimalism and Decluttering are the initial steps that help you identify beneficial investments to lead a life without exploiting resources.

Seven Keys That Will Help You Identify Your Enough for a Minimalistic Lifestyle

Understanding your "enough" requires patience and critical analysis to find balance and contentment with what you have without being stressed about owning more.

Seven keys that will help you refine your perspective of enough are:

* **Key 1**

Identify what matters most to you. Focus on your core values in terms of relationships, work, health, and creativity. The sectors that drive you to lead a fulfilled life. Now align the major sectors of your life with your long-term goals to analyze if owning more items helps you get closer to your primary goals or rather creates a distraction.

Everybody loves to own what they desire but to reach your ultimate goal you need to establish boundaries of owning and investing in items that are essential for your growth.

* **Key 2**

Assess your expenditure. When we work for a 9 to 5 job, the want to socialize becomes a need especially if you work in the corporate industry. As a result, we often pick up hobbies and sports just to maintain social relationships, and before we realize these activities develop into flawed habits that demand expensive purchases.

Golf kits to tag and impress the boss at off-duty meetings. Souvenirs to exchange with people after every trip, new dresses for after-work office parties, new household items for every house gathering, etc.

If you take a moment and pay attention to the amount of time you spend on purchasing items by convincing yourself with the idea that it helps you keep up with your desired lifestyle, you will find half of the purchases do not serve you profoundly. It is just a bad habit that has kept you hooked on buying more items.

* **Key 3**

When you buy home decorative items ask yourself if every space in your home gets utilized every day. Some people often buy identical couches, color-coordinated shelves, three dining tables, and innumerable compact pieces of furniture to fill up each spare room and vacant space in their house.

Every dining space in your home does not need a dining table to flaunt. Be creative with your décor and only buy items that you use regularly.

* **Key 4**

While in a mental rut, try to organize and declutter an area. The practice of regularly decluttering a space that contains a combination of your essentials and nonessential items makes you realize that your worth is never measured through your possessions. It was your words and your behavior toward others that helped you build heartfelt relationships.

* **Key 5**

Set mini boundaries for yourself. Make a habit of not scrolling through the media, as soon as you wake up, skip advertisements of items that allure you, and avoid the weekend sales once every 2 weeks to refrain from impulsive purchases.

When you set mini-limitations or boundaries for yourself, you not only force your mind to become disciplined but also modify your perspective toward establishing better goals. Digital clutter leads to overwhelming stress.

* **Key 6**

Build a gratitude mindset. Every time you find yourself in the conundrum of purchasing a specific item, stop and take a moment to analyze if there is a similar item in your home that you are grateful to own. Something dear to you, which if lost can or cannot be replaced with this specific one. This technique is best for incorporating the well-known magazine-friendly one-in-one-out rule. The drawback of the one-in-one-out rule is the frequency of purchasing varies from person to person.

Most of the time, the rate of purchase is much higher than the speed of discarding. This is why applying these rules to items that bewitch you to make a hefty spend is much more practical. If the new item cannot replace any of the old items that you possess dearly, do not invest a single penny in it. If it can discard any identical or nonidentical equally valuable item from your home. Try to analyze its practicality and frequency of use in your preferred lifestyle and then invest in it.

* **Key 7**

At every phase of your life the definition of your enough will change. There will be moments when you will feel content about owning only the necessary items essential for survival and there will be days when a specific sector of your life will compel you to expand your vision.

But in every phase, you will be able to determine the right limit for yourself. By choosing to stay present and practice mindful purchasing you will be able to reach your 'enough' that leads to greater freedom, clarity, and peace of mind.

The Five Psychological Issues that May Hamper Choice Efficacy

Household cleaning and implementing major changes in the crucial sectors of your life is a daunting task for every individual. However, people with underlying psychological issues can struggle more than usual in completing basic tasks. It's easy for general people to comment that what is so hard to follow a bulleted to-do list but people with ADHD and other psychological issues truly understand the overwhelming feeling that comes gift-packed to keep pace with the unending chore list.

Psychological issues are not minor health problems. One must seek professional care rather than depend on word of mouth. Every individual develops a unique perspective throughout their life. You might relate to someone who has been in the same direful situation as you to experience and feel the difficulty and pain that you have gone through. But oftentimes, the outcome and degree of suffering vary from individual to individual.

Undiagnosed psychological issues impair one's ability to focus, stay organized, and manage pressure, leading to chaos in the home and a cycle of unfinished tasks that exacerbate stress and anxiety.

When we look at messy spaces our minds feel perplexed to see each clutter individually. As a result, we feel as if we are dealing with a heap of waste that might drown us before we can see our floors hygienic, desk ordered, trash empty, clothes laundered, wardrobe organized, kitchen clean, and mail sorted.

It is best not to treat psychological issues as an obstacle in completing your daily chores but as a part of your life that, if dealt with strategically, can improve and enhance your task-handling ability.

General people can also benefit through the following methods if they are contemplating dealing with a mountain of unattended trash. Following these techniques does not alter the framework of your brain but rather equips you with streamlined household practices.

Applying these easy-to-use bite-sized tricks will not only optimize domestic routines but also keep you on top of your household chores, contributing to your physical and mental order.

Here are some ways to deal with clutter while being a neurodivergent and coping with depression. There are several more that affect choice efficacy, however, the ones that are discussed here are some that can be managed with these techniques if not in the chronic stage.

OCD, ADHD, Depression, Bipolar Disorder, and Post Traumatic Stress Disorder.

Attention Deficit Hyperactivity Disorder: If you have noticed, throughout this book many of the techniques, I have shared are ADHD-friendly. People who are diagnosed with ADHD face troubles in managing routines, organizing, beginning and finishing a task, etc.

A few months ago, when social media was flooding with trending reels of people posting content with the tagline 'I have ADHD, of course, I do this and that' I realized that I am one of those fortunate who have been struggling with this disease for an unknown number of years and later understood it was not a misconception that I have developed by consuming those quick dopamine content.

The psychological disorder ADHD has been around for decades, and the rise of social media helped to spread awareness of this disease in recent years. If you look online, you see people claiming that in the past doctors often shared that the rate of boys being affected with ADHD is higher than girls due to their fidgety, impulsive behavior. However, because of the vast exposure of media, many people's brains are adapted to believe that they might have been carrying the disease as an underlying issue.

At first, I thought I had just been brainwashed with the trend but the more I delved deeper into the topic the more sense it made. Among all the symptoms of ADHD, one major issue of ADHD-stricken people is they lose interest frequently or tend to stick to the same work for hours.

As a result, no matter how manageable those sticky to-do lists may look, striking out each point is more difficult than actual house cleaning.

The Five Things method coined by author KC Davis can simplify your approach to begin and finish tasks, switch between paired chores, and stay on track with your to-do lists. This method is impactful because it helps the brain to know what exactly needs to be done instead of being overwhelmed by the scrap heap.

According to KC Davis, whichever room you pick there are only five things that need your attention to make household chores doable.

Trash | Dishes | Laundry | Things that have a place and are not in their place | Things that do not have a place and are best to be discarded.

When you start cleaning, the first step is to take a trash bag and throw away all the trash items that are visible without much effort, damaged cardboard boxes, empty snack packets, food debris, expired cosmetic products, plastic cups, use and throw straws, chocolate wrappers, broken bits of art and crafts, used toiletries, bubble wraps, Styrofoam, used batteries, outdated medications, disposables, broken chargers, tethered wires et. cetera.

Pile them inside the trash bag and keep them aside without taking the trash out.

The second step is to pick up all the greasy dishes and pile them in the sink without washing them.

Third, gather all the scattered dirty clothes in your home and keep them inside the laundry basket without laundering them.

As a fourth step, KC Davis suggests picking a spot in your room and organizing the misplaced items in it but to make it more effective, start with the area you used more, like your work desk. Return every misplaced item to its place and separate every other item that does not belong there.

Once done, the fifth step is to pile all the items that do not have a designated place in your home and analyze if they are important objects and the frequency at which you would need those items Assign a specific place if it is important, if not throw it in the trash bag.

These steps are crucial as they eliminate the excess and make the place look ordered in minimal time. Once you complete following these five steps take out the trash, put the clothes into the laundry, and scrub off the greasy plates.

Another benefit of choosing this technique is the frequent change of pace in following the five steps keeps us up with the momentum of dealing with tasks without getting sidetracked.

Even if you lose motivation after taking the trash out, you still have already dealt with one major task that could be the root cause of health issues, emptying the trash bin. Cleaning greasy plates can come next if you still feel motivated.

Do not set schedules to clean a space in your room, instead use the timer techniques, I have shared before. Having a routine that has a specific room or category of clutter each day to tackle makes us feel uninterested and tired easily.

I tried, created, and formulated a bunch of routines but never could maintain them for more than an hour.

It is far better to quickly jot down a few tasks that you need to tackle on an urgent basis to prevent forgetting them if your attention diverts. Bite-sized to-do lists with three to four tasks are better as they redirect us to what needs to be tackled first.

Only use sticky notes, when you are facing decision paralysis at choosing which tasks you should start from, coupled it with the ABCDE method if you cannot retain information as you make progress in cleaning. Do not make it a habit of using sticky notes for every minor chore as those loose squared papers will end up being a complimentary waste and a headache for you in your next cleaning session.

Always remember, washed clothes are better than ironed ones. You can always choose to quickly press an apparel in the hour of need but do not procrastinate or chase perfectionism. I always have to remind myself that, a household chore does not demand perfection, it demands to be completed.

Even if you have cleaned the dishes and not put them away in kitchen cabinets, there is no harm in it. Eventually, they will be used again for meal preparation, and during the periodic energy outburst, those dishes will be the first to return to their chosen home.

One last tip for every ADHDer, please never keep cleaning equipment stored away from plain eyesight. The phrase out of sight, out of mind was probably quoted by

John Heywood Woorkes after befriending an ADHDer. [Jesting]

The amount of motivation, determination, and mental energy needed to take out those neatly stacked vacuum cleaners, mops, and bleach bottles from the last row of the cupboard can never be summoned even if we become mysterious superheroes. It is best to decide on an accessible place for every regular household cleaning product like the front row of the shelf or the laundry basket beside the washing machine.

Obsessive Compulsive Disorder: Obsessive-compulsive disorders have a varied set of obsessions over repeated behaviors and actions. The most common actions and thoughts related to household cleaning are; trying to organize a place in a particular order and wiping the countertops at least 5 times to neutralize the intrusive thoughts of getting harmed or a threat.

People with OCD feel obliged to do a certain task in a particular manner that is often not practical. Washing your hands now and then, even though you have not touched a single thing, starting a task exactly at 5:55 pm or else some catastrophic event will disrupt the efficiency at work, rechecking the completed tasks at least thrice so that it gets accepted without consequence and more and more

Every thought that hampers your productivity is a thought you need to discard. The best way to deal with intrusive thoughts is to remind yourself again and again that each irrational demand your mind makes is a seed for another negative belief.

Make it a mantra for every time you catch your mind forcing you to dwell on an already-finished task. Stop and pick up a different task. Tell yourself that you will return to that previously completed task once you finish completing the new task at hand and then switch again. Repeat it as many times as needed before you can see significant progress in every category of clutter.

Once you complete going through each category, chances are you will either become exhausted for another round of re-cleaning or get a better hold of external and internal situations that trigger your stress levels.

Seeking proper professional care and regular doctor visits are mandatory to not let OCD symptoms amplify. However, this small reminder may turn out effective to keep going and not get devoured into your challenging thoughts. Try before quitting.

Depression: Depression can lead to not only emotional stress but also physical problems. Personal hygiene should be a prime focus for every individual suffering from depression.

As we go through different phases of life, our moods change like the leaves of trees in seasons, and just like trees shed their old leaves and calmly wait for new ones. Our bodies wait patiently for our minds to shift their thoughts to self-care.

Depression can be a real challenge in household cleaning since the point of having pristine surroundings when a part of your life has practically collapsed into oblivion does not seem to hold great value to invest time in.

But the dates in the calendar proceed, weeks after weeks, months after months, and days after days passed as we try to figure out the reason to live.

The best way to deal with the urge to not move a muscle or do a chore is to focus on personal hygiene. When you shift your focus to personal hygiene only, the array of household chores instantly diminishes leaving us with hardly a countable task to deal with.

Although, personal hygiene may seem much more meaningless yet forcing yourself to brush your teeth once every day is a little less daunting than conducting a house cleaning marathon.

Do not divide a task into mini steps, focus on one single task as a whole, like brushing your teeth, changing your clothes, and taking a bath.

The steps related to these three personal hygiene methods are mostly done without any conscious effort so completing them is much easier than choosing what to cook, shopping for ingredients, planning meals, counting calories, preparing meals, serving, and finally eating your food.

When we make an effort every day to keep ourselves hygienic by taking a hot shower or a cold, the cells in our body get charged and relaxed which further improves our sleep.

Have you ever felt anxious and frustrated and then had a meal and all of a sudden, your anger melted? Just like food nourishes the cells in our body, taking a warm or cold bath recharges our mind from the slumber state making us feel active and at ease.

Warm baths are best for relaxation so if you are having a hard time catching sleep, try taking a warm water bath instead of a cold one. Similarly, if you feel drained, taking a cold bath can improve your energy levels.

Personal hygiene is key, to begin with your cleaning journey as when we feel at ease with ourselves, our minds try to bring order to our surroundings and urge us to clear away the clutter. If you struggle to keep up with it regularly.

Try different approaches like only focusing on brushing for a week. After a week of brushing, try to do another similar task with brushing such as washing your face using a face wash and so on. Complete it for the sake of getting rid of a task.

Post-Traumatic Stress Disorder (PTSD): Individuals with PTSD suffer from fear-stricken decisions. Deciding to do a task or choosing not to do it due to the trauma surrounding it.

Trauma can occur at any stage of our lives, but the most obstinate one is childhood trauma. Many of us grew up with parents whose way of punishment used to make us clean the dishes, fill the water bottles, organize our bookshelves, or do other no-brainer household chores if we failed to behave or needed a fix in our challenging actions, responses, or reactions.

"If you don't pick up the toys after playing, you will have no steak at dinner."

"If you don't clean your room before lunch, you will be grounded for 2 weeks"

A shared pair of words among most parents. Even though for some of us this has been a sweet nostalgic memory, many children go through unimaginable torture in the name of punishment for exterminating behavior difficulty.

Cleanliness as a tool for behavior fixing can never come under good parenting, if you want to instill good habits of organizing, hygiene, and tidying in your child, make it a game rather than a punishment. Children love to play, any activity that is fun to do and keeps them active mentally and physically.

Scattering clothes to find their Ben-10 T-shirt to wear on school trips, spilling milk with a snort because they cannot control laughing at a silly thing, and leaving their un-favorite toys on the ground because they are restricted from having a place in their new toy bucket are memories, you as a parent will hold dearly once they grow up.

Try creative games to subside clutter heap, play their favorite song, and ask them to complete an easy chore before the song finishes. Once they return from a school trip, chat about how their friends reacted to seeing their BEN-10 T-shirt, and make them understand the importance of storing it properly so that they can flaunt them again. When organizing their closet, make it a puzzle game for them to find and keep similar shapes and colors of clothes in two separate piles and teach them the right way to fold each clothes.

If your child likes to play pretend or is competitive use timers to make it a cleaning marathon or weave them a story of a clutter monster that they as a superhero needs to compete with. Be their sidekick and encourage them to win.

Inculcating healthy cleaning habits is crucial in children as once a child grows into an adult, keeping your house tidy becomes an obligation to do even if life seems to fall apart. The picture of an uncleaned messy room, piled up clothes, and an unattended kitchen makes us feel as if we are lacking in living our lives at the utmost.

The opposite is quite the truth, you can have a perfectly excelling career, undenied charms, and be efficient at every critical task yet struggle to manage a clean desk. Understand that the disarranged desk is a part of helping you stay on top of your game, don't treat it as a foe but as a friend by organizing it when you take a break.

Avoid beating yourself up mentally when you clean rather treat it as a technique of meditation and channelizing your thoughts. There's no other healthy method that can give you significant results from your hard work as instantly as wiping countertops.

Specific smells, tastes, sights, and sounds can trigger serious post-traumatic stress as they may bring flashbacks, nightmares, or feelings of intense anxiety that lead to grave mental and physical issues. Try to avoid odors, flavors, or shapes of bottles and cleaning equipment that are alarming to you.

Switch it with an odorless cleaning solution, paint your equipment with your favorite color, and try to create happy memories by tagging a friend, or playing your favorite music as you begin your tidying marathon.

Post Traumatic Stress Disorders take years to heal and still, the chances of repercussions are unpredictable. Don't shy away to reach out for help.

Bipolar Disorder: Bipolar disorder is tricky to deal with due to the frequent episodes of mood changes that make decision-making an enemy for the individual.

People with bipolar disorder should break big tasks into smaller chunks and wait for at least 48 hours before taking up a bigger house project.

During the phase of depression try focusing on no-brainer tasks like keeping yourself hygienic whereas during hypo-mania or mania phase focus on completing the critical chores.

Try to get the help of a friend or a family member to talk yourself out of all-or-nothing thinking patterns. It's okay if you cannot complete a chore within an hour, try to complete it within 3 hours or more but don't leave it undone.

Some chores are better half-done. Having a swept floor is better than a dusty one, having your seasonal clothes sorted is better than a completely messy closet, throwing wrappers in a dustbin is better than scattering them around the house, having a sparkling toilet seat is much more hygienic than a dirty one, and washing your daily wear s better than leaving them in the pile of dirty clothes near the washing machine.

Figure out which chores are essential to create order in your home and only focus on those categories of clutter. Sticky notes can be helpful if you want little dopamine shots throughout your cleaning process. Striking tasks from your list of chores can provide a sense of accomplishment to keep going.

House Cleaning Services: Pros and Cons

Outsourcing cleaning tasks to home cleaning services and scheduling regular tidying appointments is an option preferred by many individuals. Hiring a cleaning agent is a time-friendly method to eliminate long-standing clutter.

Taking the help of expert strategies of a professional can reduce the burden of tidying, delete stress, improve decision-making, and make cleaning customizable for each household.

However, like any important decision, depending on a third person to make your home immaculate needs critical weighing of advantages and disadvantages. The promise of a spotless home can be tempting when you have a schedule that forces you to race against time. Yet there are potential downsides that can lead to risky situations.

The inconsistencies of house visits, letting strangers enter your home premises every month, and depending on the reliability and trustworthiness could further contribute to decision fatigue and futile stress.

Going through genuine reviews, talking to existing customers, asking in your neighborhood about the best services in your town or city, and comparing prices of different agencies might become a tedious task in the initial phase but once you carefully vet your options, you can yield long-term benefits.

CHAPTER 7:

A COMPREHENSIVE CHECKLIST TO DECLUTTER

Now that, you have finally made your way through the last chapters of this book. I thought of sharing checklists instead of lengthy end notes with you. Having been surrounded by non-readers, I understand how much patience it takes to re-read an entire book to find out that one key point that you thought of implementing once you complete this book.

Here is a personalized index on decluttering for your every revisit.

Pairing Similar Tasks & Prioritizing Needs Over Wants

Do not differentiate each task. Become a matchmaker of chores and deal with two similar tasks at once. Identify which pair of chores needs your immediate attention and finish dealing with it first before moving to the next pair of tasks. Here is a quick list to help you identify similar tasks in your household.

Daily-Dating Chores	Weekly Dating Chores
Meal Times + Dish Cleaning	Vacuuming Furniture + Organizing Shelf
Making Bed + Decluttering Your Desk	Taking out The Trash + Cleaning the Containers
Picking Toys + Vacuuming Rooms	Watering Plants + Plucking the Dead Leaves.
Wiping Countertops + Mopping Floors	Laundering Clothes + Organizing Closet

Monthly Dating Chores	Seasonal Dating Chores
Organizing Bills + Clipping Them	Laundering Seasonal Clothes + Packing Off Season Ones
Cleaning rugs + Vacuuming Carpets	Mowing the lawn + Sweeping the Porch
Wiping Mirrors + Scrubbing Windows	
Bathroom Floors + Toilet Clean	

Role of Timers & The Power of Pre-Breaks

- Using a timer to complete a chore is effective for making significant progress in short intervals. Set a short timer for 15-25 minutes to keep yourself on track.
- If you are an individual who prefers to work from home or during weekends, take a short five to ten minutes pre-lunch and pre-dinner break and organize each misplaced item in your home. Only focus on trivial tasks such as filling empty water bottles, organizing your daily wear, and watering your indoor plants. This is one of the most effective and my favorite ways to keep the cleaning ball rolling and reduce each week's tidying load effectively.

The Five Alphabet Approach

The International Best Seller author Brian Tracy's 'Five Alphabet Approach' can not only help you in tackling office work but also help you identify urgent clutter quickly. Here is a detailed description of implementing the ABCDE approach in your household chores.

- **Letter A:** The most critical waste that needs your immediate attention.
- **Letter B:** Household chores that you must finish by the end of the day.
- **Letter C:** Extra chores that will make you feel a little more productive.
- **Letter D:** Delegate easy tasks to your family.
- **Letter E:** Tasks that you can eliminate.

Make it a Family Event & Sort by Category, Not Location!

Take help from your family or roommates and assign no-brainer tasks to each of them to undertake critical chores. When you declutter your house, do not opt for room-by-room cleaning. Instead, sort your clutter by category, not location. Here is the correct order recommended by Author Marie Kondo to sort items at your home.

Clothes | Books | Papers | Komono | Mementos

Clothes: The secret of an organized closet is in the space-saving folding techniques for each piece of apparel.

Books: Divide your collection of books into fiction and non-fiction and focus on the lesser pile first. Every book you choose to keep must benefit your present self.

If it's a nonfiction book, analyze the value of the advice shared in the book. If it is a fiction book explore the ideas and see if the main character's story compels you to switch roles, with it.

Papers: Divide the paper into six further categories and rely on the importance of the information the paper contains followed by the frequency you would be needing it. Here is a quick list of the six categories.

Category 1: Financial Documents: Financial Documents are Bank Statements, Credit Card Statements, Mortgage or Lease Agreements, Investment Statements, Tax returns, Pay Stubs, Insurance Policies, Property Tax Bills, Utility Bills, Receipts, and Loan Documents.

Category 2: Household and Property: Household and Property will contain Home Improvements, Contracts and

Receipts, Home Inventory Records, Appliance Manuals, Home Warranty Information, Property Deeds and Titles, Rental Agreements, and HOA Documents.

Category 3: Personal and Legal Documents: Personal and Legal Documents are Birth Certificates, Wills and Trusts, Power of Attorney Documents, Social Security Card Documents, Marriage Licenses, Passports, Driver Licenses, Adoption Papers, Divorce Decrees, and Military Records.

Category 4: Medical and Health Documents: Medical and Health Documents are Insurance Cards, Immunization Records, Dental Records, Vision Care Records, Medical Bills, Prescription Records, and Health Insurance Policies.

Category 5: Children and Education: The Children and Education section will have School Records, Report Cards, Vaccination Records, Extracurricular Activity Records, College Applications, and Financial Aid Documents.

Category 6: Miscellaneous: Miscellaneous contains documents such as Receipts of Electronics, Magazines, Newspapers, Flyers, Warranties, Guarantees, Manuals, Coupons, and Sticky Notes.

Komono: Komono items are every unspecific and unidentified object you come across while cleaning your house. Only keep those items that are functional and discard every item that you cannot use today, tomorrow, or within three to six months.

The best way to sort this diverse section is by grouping them into broader categories such as:

- Pen drives & Flash drives
- Skin Care Products
- Makeup & Cosmetics
- Accessories
- Valuables like passports, credit cards, social security cards, loose change, etc.
- Digital cameras, appliances, electronics, cords, and unidentified parts of products.
- Household Supplies: Toilet papers, disposables, cleaning equipment, etc.
- Kitchen Kits: Kitchen goods, foil papers, plastic wraps, etc.

Mementos: Use containers for storing mementos and limit yourself to a specific number of containers to escape hoarders' bait.

Breaking the Generational Trauma of Clutter

Do not shift your unneeded keepsakes from one room to another. Throw out every keepsake that sparks the idea of sending it to your parent's home or donating it to your siblings.

Baby Toys and Pet Care

Although this section can use an entire chapter writing the essence of furry pets or the bliss of having children around is quite a common topic in every decluttering book.

So, remembering the points included in this checklist is much more beneficial and time-efficient for your household needs.

When it comes to toys for babies and furry pets. Do a routine cleaning every week. Pets and children lose interest in toys quite often. It's better to set a specific day once every two to three weeks to understand which toys no longer satisfy your baby's needs or have been tethered by your pet.

In my home, the practice of getting limited toys to each pet was an established rule even before I was born. All the dogs that my family has ever owned have only one or two material items that they played with. When I grew up and bought a dog, he was also limited to two chewing balls. All the other tethered items that I brought in his baby years are discarded.

When it comes to baby toys throw out every broken toy that your baby does not show interest in. You can include your child for effective organizing and decision-making. They can help you figure out which toys make them truly happy and for which toys they want a replacement.

When it comes to baby gear, opt for multifunctional pieces of equipment, like a baby crib that can be converted into a baby bed or a high chair that transitions into a booster seat. If you are still hoarding baby items even after your child has moved out of your house. It's better to let them go. Choose one small item that brings back happy memories, not giant items that eat up your storage space.

When it comes to pet fur, rather than spending paycheck after paycheck to buy identical fur removal tools, it is best to invest some bucks in purchasing pet-friendly furniture and grooming your pet regularly without fail.

Every furry friend deserves a spa treatment but not all furry friends need it. A simple regular habit of brushing the coat, bathing, and trimming the nails is enough to maintain your pet's charms and reduce extra waste.

Set up a limited space where your baby can play with their toys, and develop habits of organizing the toys every time they are done playing.

For essential items that belong to your pet like their food bowls, water bowl, and toys. Set a pet-friendly station and train them to keep the misplaced objects in their designated place.

Embrace the Imperfection: Houses with pets and kids cannot stay immaculate 365 days or every week. There will be days when your living space might look like a whirlpool has surpassed it with scattered toys, leftover pet food, and a mound of pet fur.

Do not beat yourself up from the classic phrases of 'I'm a bad parent' or 'I cannot even maintain cleanliness in my home'. Understand that change is messy. Your children and pets are constantly growing, so try to enjoy their childhood and growing phase before it slips away from your fingertips.

A home with laughter and commotion is equally pleasing as a quiet living space.

Cobwebs and Creatures

This section is very near and dear to my heart. If you remember, in the previous chapters I shared how my current house is surrounded by canopies of trees. As beautiful as it sounds, choosing to live in this house comes with its own set of trials and tribulations.

Caterpillars, cocoons, butterflies, bees, unnamed insects, frogs, pests, crawlers, reptiles, moths, crickets, grasshoppers, ants, mosquitoes, the list will never cease. Practically it is a forest home yet to be discovered by the rangers. (Note the sarcasm)

As a result, spider nets on window grills and room ceilings can be often spotted in my home, and even though my mom discards every item that does not add value to her home when it comes to cocoons, she has developed a soft corner for them and you can often spot them sticking high on walls waiting to transform in a butterfly or moth. If I insist on cleaning, she uses her excuse that they are far away from our reach so there is no point in breaking those creatures' homes.

Over the years I have also developed a soft corner for letting butterflies and moths enter to wander around in my room. Every time they sneak in, an instant feeling of happiness spreads in my heart.

But creatures that might invite harmful diseases should be dealt with on an urgent basis. If your home is a budding ground of cockroaches, try to use sealed waste cans to throw packets of expired foods. Don't leave out food spills especially overnight, and wipe off countertops promptly after use. Store pet foods in air-tight containers and seal potential entry points window cracks, door screens, gaps, and holes to prevent them from entering.

Humidity and leaks attract pests in your home, so try to de-humidify bathrooms and other humid places using proper air ventilators and de-humidifiers.

Many people also suggest that DIY insect resistance like peppermint, lavender, eucalyptus, and tea tree oils acts as a natural insect repellent. Using vinegar and water to clean surface areas can deter ants and bugs. Placing sachets of dried herbs like bay leaves, cloves, and cinnamon sticks in the cupboard and pantry areas is said to repel insects. However, the degree of efficiency of these food items in driving harmful insects from our homes cannot be guaranteed.

You can also opt for effective insect repellent, and take the help of professionals like pest control services to prevent reinfestation and chase those creatures away.

Getting rid of harmful household insects is essential as many mosquitoes, bugs, and flies feed off large chunks of our skin that cause serious rashes and irritation. Mosquitoes are best to be killed or completely avoided as these creatures use us as their snacks to transmit grave health issues.

Downgrading Old Clothes To Dusters

In terms of house cleaning, some specific bits of advice cannot be forced to apply.

You need to decide by yourself whether to choose an advised method or go against it. Downgrading old clothes to dusters is one such advice.

The pros and cons of this method carry equal weight so abiding by it may come with challenges or prove to be beneficial.

Here are some parallels drawn to simplify your decision.

Downgrading old clothes to dusters is a cost-effective way to keep your surroundings clean but regular use may further wear off the clothes which if not managed can produce clutter.

Repurposing old clothes is an effective way to introduce and support sustainability for the environment but hygiene can often get compromised when re-using old clothes.

Torn clothes as rags are considered to be a practical approach but it can often loop you into unnecessary emotional attachments. How often did you see mothers using the same cloth for dusting even if the cloth is entirely damaged?

When we clean with an old cloth that has memories associated with it, we have a hard time letting go of that item as it acts as an aid for the lost time.

Natural fabrics and cotton clothes are effective absorbents but synthetic old clothes may lack cleaning efficiency which makes them a less ideal choice for cleaning tasks that involve water.

House Shifts Are Best To Get Rid Of Old Accumulated Waste

If you are like my family who needs to shift houses regularly, utilize this time to effectively eliminate excessive mess. Some people carry every piece of furniture, miscellaneous, old home decor, and bags and bags of clutter with them.

Treat your house shift as a farewell to the clutter built in your old place. Only choose functional items to carry to your next house.

Understand the dimensions of your new house if a specific piece of furniture will block more space than needed in your new single-room compartment, it's best to sell that item. If a piece of furniture is broken, it is better to discard it than to keep it with the hope that one day you will fix and use that item.

If you are deciding on furniture purchases for your new home. Only buy the essential items that you will need to survive conveniently. Too many identical bathroom rugs, mats for every door of your house, trinkets, unnumbered wall art, overly specialized cleaning tools, themed dinner wares, trendy smart home gadgets, duplicate furniture pieces like extra side tables, redundant chairs and fancy kitchen tools like egg slicers, avocado peelers, etc. are just free clutter of your new home.

Plan your furniture meticulously and only invest in pieces that will help you live comfortably.

CHAPTER 8:
A COMPREHENSIVE CHECKLIST TO MINIMALISM

The word minimalism is not a method of limiting waste production but a lifestyle that once achieved sets you free from the illusion of consumerism. It is a process that is both liberating and challenging. It introduces the uncertainty of possessing less and molds your perspective of contentment.

Humans are quite susceptible to the idea of owning more as it influences our status in society. It makes us look abundant, happy, prosperous, and affluent in monetary terms, but often it's quite the opposite of what we perceive.

Have you ever seen a person who leads a minimalistic life complain about having fewer items at home or in their life? They do not just appear happy, they create genuine happiness by reflecting on their goals, visualizing their ideal space, and setting realistic expectations.

Below is the checklist of the key points that I discussed in this book along with new methods and benefits that come gift-packed when you choose to lead your life with a minimalistic approach.

The Art of Mindful Purchasing

Make your purchases intentional rather than impulsive. When an item catches your attention, ask yourself, "Do you want others to see you have that specific item, or do you need it for your survival?"

This question will not only reduce your spending habits but also impact your perspective on purchasing.

Farewell to Attachments

While sorting mementos, choose items that inspire you to become your better self, not items that make you cling to memories. There is a remarkable difference between a box of dead dreams and memories that motivates you to weave new visions.

Investing In the Right Q

Being a bargain hunter for every purchase you make might help you to be fashionable for a month or two, but investing in quality over quantity will save you more time, space, and money. It is better to own an item that you can pair with ten different outfits than spending your entire paycheck each month to restock your wardrobe.

A Minimalistic Wardrobe

While picking home clothes, choose comfort over fancy. The category loungewear is designed to provide comfort not just to make you appear polished and sleek.

A great method to minimize wardrobe purchases is by incorporating only 7 sets of loungewear for homes and pairing 33 items for clothes that you style outside.

The 33 pairs must contain accessories, pieces of jewelry clothes, and shoes. Plan three months of outfits from those 33 items and seal pack the rest of the items away from sight.

This method is not only effective in deleting your decision fatigue but also in shaping your outlook towards less is more.

Incorporating the Five Elements for Reorganizing Your Home

Rooted in the Taoist philosophy, the principles of Feng Shui were traditionally used to orient buildings, particularly, homes and temples to promote health, wealth, and good fortune. Later it spread to different parts of the world which then manifested the idea of attracting energy to enhance the surroundings of our living.

The main idea of Feng Shui in terms of household revolves around channeling the energy, or Chi, and increasing the positive energy indoors.

Investing in the five elemental energies to revamp your house is a great start to incorporating the main concept of Feng Shui in your home. Focus on each element's symbolism while organizing your home to create a holistic environment for yourself.

ELEMENT	HOUSEHOLD ITEMS
WOOD	Sturdy Wooden Cabinets, Multipurpose Wardrobes, Smart beds, and an adequate number of sofas as per the needs of your home fall under the category of wood.
	Do not try to decorate every space of your home with different types of furniture. Choose to keep key furniture in a place from where you can easily see the door to maintain the flow of Chi.

FIRE	Choose bright lights over soft lights while cleaning a space. Even though Feng Shui emphasizes having natural lights for ideal space or warm lights on easy hours of the day. I believe bright lights keep us alert and energized throughout the tidying process.
EARTH	Incorporate low-maintenance indoor plants for an inviting ambiance. Plants remove toxins and keep indoor air clean. Invest in plants that survive on negligence. Dead plants in Feng Shui symbolize the draining of energy from homes, so if you are a newbie plant parent invest in one or two indoor plants in the beginning.
METAL	Opt for multifunctional cleaning tools rather than identical cleaning parts. While buying household cleaning equipment we often invest in too many items that serve us in similar ways.
WATER	Deep clean your entire house once every two months. Use manufactured cleaning solutions rather than DIY solutions. DIY solutions leave a yellow stain after prolonged use.

Shift your Focus to Gathering Experiences, not Materials

Prioritize investing your time and energy in activities that create memories such as hiking, taking short trips, and learning a new skill that does not require you to invest in materialistic possessions.

Create Open and Clean Spaces

While organizing and investing in home décor, decide your critical needs over wants. Not every space in your home demands an item to showcase.

Limit Digital Time

The screens of our gadgets are the most used spaces in our lives after our homes. Put a reminder to declutter spam emails and identical photos to keep your digital space clutter-free.

I build a habit of setting a quick 5-minute timer and sorting out important emails with the unimportant ones before I start my work.

If you struggle to use an app efficiently, ask for help from a person or look for solutions online.

Scan Documents

Another great way to keep paper clutter at bay is by scanning and saving shareable documents. Not all the documents in your workspace need a physical copy. Analyze and keep or discard.

Build a Functional Kitchen

Kitchens are the places in our homes, that often complicates us in terms of necessary items. You will find yourself choosing each piece of knife because it promises or cut vegetables differently.

All the cookie cutters come in varied shapes further prompting us to choose our children's current favorite. To analyze the importance of kitchen kits, focus in terms of multifunctionality.

Do not buy identical sets of the same items. Understand your cooking needs and invest in items that you will regularly use. Items that are used rarely can be purchased as per the demand of the situation.

Set a Rule of 30 Days for Every Unnecessary Purchase

There will be times when the question 'Do you want the item for survival?' might not be enough to convince you not to purchase it. In those convoluting times, wait for 30 days, if the desire or the thought of the item remains along with a valid reason go for it and if there is no functional reason, don't invest in the item.

Choose Neutral Colors for Home Décor

Although I do not believe the idea of incorporating neutral tones in your room walls gives a sense of peace and serenity. But I do believe that lighter colors make the room look spacious and clean. Neutral colors like beige, light gray, and white reflect the light in your room better than darker shades of colors.

Minimize Social Commitments

Once you become a minimalist, you will refine your skill of saying **'NO'** or refusing plans that you are uninterested in. Many people often struggle with denying requests, be it from a loved one or an acquaintance.

The desperate need to please the other party becomes an unescapable trap for us. A minimalistic mindset helps you not only identify calendar obligations but also prioritize social engagements aligning you with people that bring absolute joy to you.

Make the Concept of Daily Routine Digestible

When you aspire to bring significant changes in your life, establishing a habitual routine becomes an obstacle to reaching your goals. A minimalistic mindset helps you simplify your approach toward achieving a goal and increases productivity by establishing a productive routine through critical thinking.

Build Better Relationships

Minimalist people do not dwell on futile attachments, as a result, they are often found building relationships that remain for longer periods.

They invest their time in cultivating strong, meaningful bonds and choose fewer close ones. When we understand the true meaning of every relationship and the dynamic ways each relationship serves us, we cherish the bonds that we make.

This further reduces the baggage of emotional investments and the desperate want to please other people who do not add value to our lives.

Have a No-Spare Rule

If you are thinking of starting your minimalistic journey, the moment you finish reading this book, start by implementing a no-spare rule. Every loose item, you come across, or extra gadgets, kitchen kits, or toiletries build a habit of eliminating rather than sulking in your 'just because' or 'just in case' thoughts.

This method will further reduce unnecessary backup clutter on your next tidying sessions.

CONCLUSION

The chance encounter between you and me and the journey of this book ends here. But your expedition to a tranquil oasis begins.

Thank you for investing your time and reading this book. I hope the methods, techniques, and tricks you learned help you make better purchases in the future and eradicate the stress of clutter.

There's more to life than paying one EMI after another.

Always remember that minimalism and decluttering aren't just a house management process. It is a journey of finding your true self. The beautiful person that you are inside out.

When I started writing this book, I felt skeptical about how I would be able to write such a vast number of words on a topic over which thousands of books have already been published.

What more would I add to a house cleaning book that creates value and helps people live a fulfilled life?

But now that I have finished writing this book, I realized how grateful and contented I feel to share my own story about struggling with the necessities, and the difficulties I have faced, which other people could relate to.

The hardships we go through in making our homes immaculate do not define our strength. It is the choices we make that help us understand our true potential.

If you could relate to any situation or gain at least one insight from this book, I would believe that the book has fulfilled its intention. You can choose to discard it once you finish reading this book but before that make sure to embark on the journey of decluttering and minimalism.

Make sure to take a chance to rediscover yourself. You will be amazed by the aftereffects the idea of less brings in obtaining more in life.

If you can invest in impulsive purchases, also try meaningful investments. Our homes are our ultimate destination in life. No matter how far we travel, how high we climb the ladder of success, or how advanced society becomes, houses will always be a constant source of shelter and protection.

Build a home that invites you to stay, not a house that drives you away.
....

Also, if you are still curious about the bitter item I accidentally ate at my aunt's house, it was a seed of the vegetable parwal that transformed me from a packrat to a neatnik.

CONCLUSION

If a small seed can help me alter my entire life aligning me to true abundance and prosperity. Imagine the profound change it can bring when you consciously put efforts into implementing the knowledge you have acquired. Try to become a friend rather than your own enemy.

Your house needs you as much as you need it. Only you possess the power to befriend your life and drive a radical transformation.

Empower yourself by first nurturing the place that keeps you protected and safe.

Jacqueline D. Austin

Printed in Great Britain
by Amazon